MW00816667

TEDBooks

! *or* ?

TED Books
Simon & Schuster

New York   London   Toronto   Sydney   New Delhi

Judge

this.

CHIP KIDD

Simon & Schuster, Inc.
1230 Avenue of the Americas
New York, NY 10020

TED, the TED logo, and TED Books are trademarks of
TED Conferences, LLC.

First TED Books hardcover edition June 2015

TED BOOKS and colophon are registered trademarks of
TED Conferences, LLC.

SIMON & SCHUSTER and colophon are registered
trademarks of Simon & Schuster, Inc.

For information about special discounts for
bulk purchases, please contact Simon & Schuster
Special Sales at 1-866-506-1949 or
business@simonandschuster.com.

For information on licensing the TED Talk that
accompanies this book, or other content partnerships
with TED, please contact TEDBooks@TED.com.

Cover and interior design by Chip Kidd
Photographs of Good's packaging by Geoff Spear

Manufactured in the United States of America

10 9 8 7 6 5 4 3 2 1

ISBN 978-1-4767-8478-6
ISBN 978-1-4767-8479-3 (ebook)

For J. D. McClatchy

All photographs by Chip Kidd,
using an iPhone 5S, unless otherwise noted.

"Early impressions are hard to eradicate
from the mind. When once wool
has been dyed purple,
who can restore it
to its previous whiteness?"
—*Saint Jerome,*
AD 331–420

"Let me make one thing perfectly clear."
—*Richard M. Nixon*

"God was always invented to explain mystery."
—*Richard P. Feynman*

So,

what is your first impression of this book?

Well, you're still reading, so it couldn't have been that bad.

Or at least it was intriguing enough.

First impressions are key to how we perceive the world, and are perceived by it. They are our introductions to everything: acquaintances, the workplace, products, experiences, retail stores, the Internet, entertainment, relationships, design. And based on our first impressions, we judge things. We can't help it. Does that sound terrible? We all heard it as children: "Don't judge by appearances." But we do, because we live in a visual culture, and our minds instantly react to what we see.

What really matters is not *that* we judge, but *how* we do so. Is it with intelligence? Empathy? Compassion?

If you consider the example of design, the "don't judge" rule doesn't even make sense. Design, by its very nature, demands to be judged when you initially encounter it, because it is supposed to solve a problem. And if that's not happening . . . that's a problem.

How many forms have you had to fill out that are needlessly complicated? How many websites have you been directed to that you can't figure out how to use? Indeed, the Web is all *about* first impressions, and the need to be able to understand content at first glance.

As a graphic designer, specifically a designer of book covers, I'd say that making a great first impression is not just my interest, it's my job. Whether it's ink on paper or pixels on a screen, a book cover is not only the face of the text, it's your primary connection to it.

But you don't need to be a designer to appreciate problem-solving: whether you are a social worker dealing with government forms, a doctor analyzing medical data, a Web coder, or even a barista trying to figure out the espresso machine, you can tell when a piece of design is working for you or not.

I've found that the two most effective and fascinating aspects of first impressions—both the ones I create and those I encounter—are at opposite ends of the spectrum: Clarity and Mystery. After more than thirty years as a practicing designer, I continue to be amazed by how these two components work, and what happens when they get mixed up or misused.

And wow, do they. Politicians can be some of the most mysterious people in the world, usually when we need them to be the clearest. And in the age of Too Much Information, we've all seen things that could benefit from a little more mystery (that family with a name that starts with a *K* comes to mind).

So let's begin with two questions. First:

When should you be clear?

That depends on the message you want to get across, and its nature. You should be clear when you need people to understand you immediately. You want others to be clear when you need vital and specific information—say, technical guidance for your computer or phone, or when you're lost and you ask someone for directions. In either case, what is needed is clarity, and when it's not there we all know the results can be very frustrating. Especially when your GPS cuts out.

A more extreme but not uncommon example is when you hear recordings of 911 calls on the news. I always think, "If I were taking the call, would I be able to understand what the situation is?" The answer varies, and of course the calls are usually made in moments of intense panic, but these are definitely situations when a person needs to be understood.

If we apply this idea to design in our everyday lives, the examples start to become, well, clear:

Highway signage. Instruction manuals. Alarm clocks. Emergency escape routes. Wedding vows.

When decoration—a pretty facade, ornamentation, elaboration—really doesn't matter at all, clarity is most needed.

Clarity is sincere, direct, reasonable, basic, honest, perfectly readable.

No-nonsense.

But when it's automatically applied to everything, things can get kind of boring.

Now, let's look at the yin to this yang, and ask:

When should you be mysterious?

Ah, the allure of Mystery. And the fun of it. Or, if we're not careful, the disappointment of it. Mystery is an extremely powerful tool; just ask Gypsy Rose Lee (kids, do a Web search) or the creators of *Lost*. You should be mysterious when you want to get people's attention and hold it, when you want your audience to work harder—when, frankly, you have something to hide.

Mystery is: a puzzle that demands to be solved, a secret code you want to crack, an illusion that may not be an illusion at all, a dream you're trying to remember before it fades away.

Mystery, it must be said, can also be terrifying: phantom pain, sudden change, irrational behavior, the loss of power. The threat of the unknown.

In my own work, mystery is hugely important. I design covers for all kinds of books: fiction, nonfiction, poetry, history, memoir, essay, comics. Each demands its own visual approach. Sometimes I want the viewer to "get it" right away, but more often I want to intrigue him or her enough to investigate the book further (i.e., to open it up, begin to read it, and hopefully buy it).

Mystery, by its very nature, is much more complex than clarity, and I try to create a balance between the two.

So for the purposes of this book, I'm introducing . . .

The Mysteri-o-meter.

The field of Information Graphics has certainly progressed over the last several decades (thank you, *USA Today*, for the charts and graphs). The idea is to create a visual piece of communication that can be understood in any languange. The "Mysteri-o-meter" on the opposite page is an example of that: a simple scale that marks the balance between Clarity (**!**) and Mystery (**?**)—the former at 1, and the latter at 10—and I've applied it to all the visual examples in the book.

Note: When something is at one extreme of the scale or the other, it doesn't necessarily mean it's good or bad. As with just about everything in life, you'll have to take this caveat in context. Some examples will be frustratingly mysterious when they should be clear, and some will be all too clear when more discretion is wanted. And vice versa.

And so, let's start with the process of . . .

CLARITY   1   2   3   4   5   6   7   8   9   10   MYSTERY

Learning to judge.

I am often asked "What inspires you?" and "When you have a creative block, how do you unblock it?" The unhelpful answer to the first question is that I can be inspired by just about everything, both good and bad. But when you have a problem to solve—whether it's fixing a leak, keeping deer out of your yard, or trying to mend a broken relationship—your inspiration, your first clue about what to do, lies within an analysis of the problem itself. That's where the solution originates.

As for a creative block, my psychic Drano, so to speak, is my environment and the things and people in it. I am lucky enough to live and work in Manhattan, and when I'm stuck, I have only to walk two or three blocks in any direction and I'm instantly reminded of the resilience of humanity and our ability to create things in the face of massive indifference and mounting expense. You see examples of design that astound (MoMA, the Chrysler Building, Central Park), some that are a disaster (subway passages that are too small to handle commuter crowds, taxi off-duty lights, poorly demarked sidewalks suddenly closed for construction), and everything in between.

But you don't need to be a New Yorker or a designer to appreciate how things are created and how they function in the world. You just have to be interested. And yes, you have to judge, often based on a first impression. Why not learn how to do it better?

I am going to show you some examples of objects and places that form my ideas about design and how it can work, or not. I encounter them in my life every day, and have taken all the following pictures myself.

Let's start with one that's very simple and often overlooked:

Help me organize
my life, please.

If you work in publishing, you will have discovered binder clips very quickly. They hold literally everything together, from manuscripts to page proofs, and I've found them to be an invaluable organizational tool.

For those of you who don't work in publishing, I urge you to get some binder clips regardless. The simplicity and elegance of these devices is utterly transparent, as opposed to, say, digital folders within folders within folders. And the handles of the clip can be collapsed down so that they lie flat.

Whenever I go on a trip (once a month on average), I print out all applicable documents—boarding passes, itineraries, hotel reservation codes, rental car papers, etc.—and collect them in a single bundle with a color-coded binder clip. I drop the bundle in my tote bag (with the clip visible at the top—this is very important) and I'm off. When I need the documents, they can be located immediately by the bright hue of the clip.

As for storing all this stuff on your phone, news flash: your phone can die. Paper does not die, because it's already dead and resurrected.

I remember being caught in a security line at JFK behind a gentleman (ahem) who was trying in vain to revive his smartphone to show his boarding pass, to no avail. There were tears.

First impression: Squeeze, clamp, release. Organized.

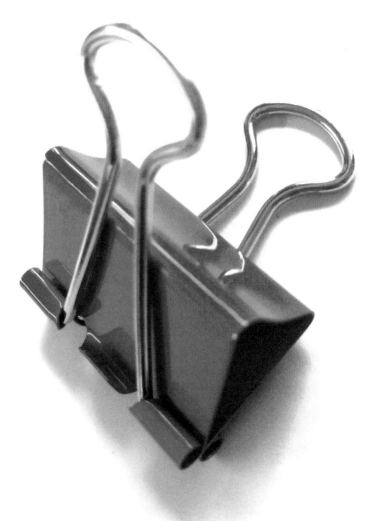

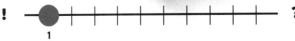

! 1 ?

Nice package.

As long as there are consumer goods, there will always be physical packaging. But just because something is meant to be paid for and consumed does not mean its design has to be cloying, condescending, or screaming for your attention.

The Mrs. Meyer's cleaning products are a great recent example of how this can be done distinctively and successfully. The typography is so, well, clean. The red circle with the white interior is strategically placed in the center of the label, clearly telling you what it smells like. The product itself is biodegradable and isn't tested on animals. The bottles are recyclable.

Also eye-catching and yet beautifully understated are the vessels for Good's Potato Chips. I was born and raised in southeastern Pennsylvania, and these chips were a staple of my childhood. To this day they're only distributed locally. You can get them in a two-pound cardboard box (opposite, right), but when I was a kid they used to come in big tin cans (opposite, left), which we could either return for a refill or keep for reuse. But we never threw them away. The design scheme has remained unchanged since the company was founded in 1886. Red containers are for "Homestyle" (lighter, crispier chips), and blue containers are for "Kettle Cooked" (thicker, crunchier chips).

Oh, and they're incredibly delicious because they're cooked in LARD. Oh, yes. *Burp!*

First impression: I can identify these products immediately, and high quality will make me a loyal customer.

! ——●——|——|——|——|——|——|——|——|——|—— **?**

1

Use only as directed . . . but for what?

And then there is *this* kind of packaging, for prescription medication, which baffles me. Why is it that over-the-counter medicinal packaging tells you exactly what it's for, while prescribed products do not? For example, Lamisol proudly declares that it "Kills Athlete's Foot," while my prescribed luliconazole cream, used to treat the same thing, says nothing of the kind. I asked a friend of mine in the pharmaceutical business about this, and while he didn't have a definitive answer, he did come up with a two-part theory. First, the drug industry assumes that if you are prescribed a treatment by a doctor, he or she will tell you what it's for, so the label doesn't have to. Second, the *real* story is that it's (surprise, surprise) . . . a legal issue, and has to do with diagnoses far more dire than foot fungus. Not long ago, drug giant Eli Lilly was sued because a doctor prescribed one of its products for depression when it was really meant to treat schizophrenia. It did not end well, either for the patient or the company. Such is the potential danger of mystery and interpretation.

So what's the answer? Sharpies! They write on *anything*. I can scrawl directly on tubes and pill-bottle tops in black or red ink and take away the guessing.

First impression: I need to know what a product is for, right away, just by looking at it. *Especially* medicine.

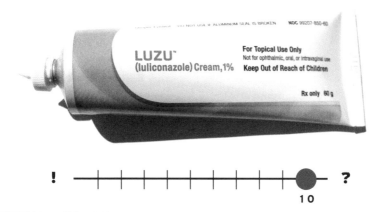

LUZU (luliconazole) Cream, 1% for topical use
Initial U.S. Approval: 2013

--------------------------------INDICATIONS AND USAGE--------------------------------

LUZU (luliconazole) Cream, 1% is an azole antifungal indicated for the topical treatment of interdigital tinea pedis, tinea cruris, and tinea corporis caused by the organisms *Trichophyton rubrum* and *Epidermophyton floccosum,* in patients 18 years of age and older. (1)

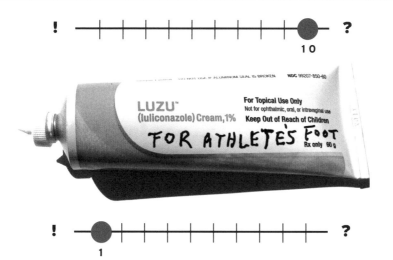

Bite.

When I heard that one of my graphic-design heroes, Peter Saville—the legendary designer for Manchester, England, label Factory Records (whose recording artists included Joy Division and New Order)—was going to redesign the iconic Lacoste crocodile (below), I was as surprised as I was delighted. Here were two of my favorite worlds—preppy clothes and post-punk music—colliding unexpectedly and deleriously head-on.

The original logo was created in the 1920s by French tennis star René Lacoste, nicknamed "The Crocodile" for his tenacity on the court. For its 2013 limited edition of the shirt, the Lacoste label hired Saville to reinterperet it, and he did so with inspired fervor. He generated eighty variations in all (opposite), commemorating the eightieth anniversary of the company. These abstractions are recognizable because we know both the source material and the context: over the heart on a white cotton polo shirt.

First impression of the original logo: Cool metaphor.

First impression of Saville's variations: Even cooler.

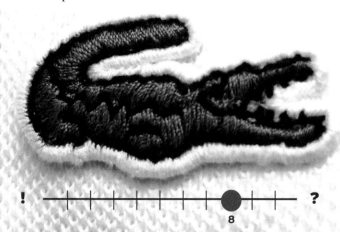

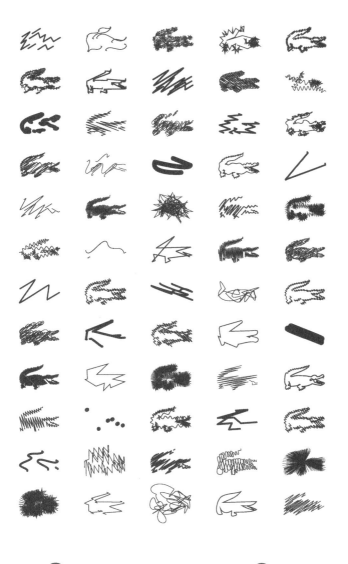

! 1 ➝ 10 ?

Block that billing!

It always seems strange to me that movie poster credits (or the billing block, as it's known in the business) appear in those extremely condensed, skinny typefaces that are so hard to read. The reason for this has to do with film industry guidelines and a typographic technicality determined by the logo of the film on the poster. Type (or font) height is measured in units called points (this text you're reading right now is 11 points, for example). Type width is not actually numerically measured at all, but is classified by "weight"—light, bold, extra bold, heavy, etc.

So, by most Hollywood labor union standards, the point size of the billing block has to be at least 25 to 35 percent of the point size of the title of the movie. Using an ultracondensed typeface allows the height of the characters to meet contractual obligations while still providing enough horizontal space to include all the required text.

And render it nearly indecipherable.

The image opposite was scanned in at actual size from an ad in the *New York Times*, and in addition to the fact that the printing is terrible (see "CMYK," page 90), the most important incidental information seems to be that it will be released on September 12 and is rated R. I think the creators should be better credited.

And by the way——as someone who sets type all the time for a living, I can tell you that using a smaller point size with a heavier width for billing blocks would be much easier to read and fit the space just fine. Like this.

First impression: Who made it?

10

Hot impression.

Manufactured by the Pyrex/Corning Glass corporation in 1945 as an attempt to save metal for the war effort, the so-called Silver Streak glass iron's beauty is matched only by its utter impracticality. It appears to embody a total contradiction of purposes, like a toaster made out of ice. And yet the result is a marvel of industrial engineering that has a reason for being beyond aesthetics, which is why I find it so inspiring—it's a mundane household appliance transformed into a work of art. It was originally available in five colors: red, blue, green, silver, and gold, and was in production for only one year. Collectors trip over themselves to get one, or do whatever the Internet equivalent of tripping over oneself is.

First impression: Familiar function, surprising form. The ordinary can be made extraordinary.

Call Security!

Of course security in Manhattan office buildings is extremely important, but what never ceases to amaze me are the instant ID tags they make for you in the lobbies of some corporations when you come to visit—in this case (opposite), DC Comics. They have a little camera mounted on the reception desk, and the person behind it takes your picture and prints out a paper ID card (full disclosure: the same thing happens at the TED offices in downtown New York City), which you use to get through the turnstiles and into the elevators.

Fine. What I take issue with is the photo. I mean, that's actually me, but it could be anybody. What's the point? They've already looked at my driver's license, and I'm logged into the visitors' list; shouldn't this technology be a little more advanced by now? Oh well, just call me the Phantom Stranger (comic-book geek joke; look it up).

First impression: If even I can't recognize myself, how is security supposed to? Are print-on-demand ID cards really still in their infancy?

So cool.

Just when you're ready to give up on the human race in general, along comes the Ice Bucket Challenge, and you believe again.

And then all your friends and Superman and Lois Lane do it, too (opposite), and you donate money.

I realize that by the time this sees print the Ice Bucket Challenge may be yesterday's news, but it's worth noting here anyway, because this is how to spread a message using a great idea—remember: polio was once yesterday's news, too. The origins of the practice of dumping cold water on one's head to raise money for charity are unclear and have been attributed to multiple sources (mostly televised football games), but this initiative, started in 2014, has raised well over $300 million to date to fund research in the fight against amyotrophic lateral sclerosis (aka ALS, or Lou Gehrig's disease), for which there is as yet no effective treatment or cure.

The idea is simple, direct, and tailor-made for the age of viral video, and emphasizes perpetuation. Perhaps most important, it connected with the public at large, who otherwise might not have been aware of the cause and were all too willing to dump freezing-cold water over their heads so they could empathize with people less fortunate than themselves.

The message took hold. We don't need to see cats riding vacuum cleaners anymore; we need to do something about a dire problem, and have some fun in the process—and pay our good fortune forward.

First impression: This is how to design a fund-raiser.

ALS Ice Bucket Challenge - Amy Adams & Henry Cavill

Cruel Films

4

Fully adjustable.

You may or may not be familiar with this side table, but the designer, Eileen Gray (1878–1976), deserves to be a household name. She is my go-to design hero for furniture and interiors, and she came to prominence after her death. Gray befriended contemporaries like Le Corbusier and Marcel Breuer, and her work was inspired by the Bauhaus, but I think she transcended that movement with just the right amount of quirk.

She was recognized by clients and the design cognoscenti of her milieu, but none of her creations were mass-produced in her lifetime, which is tragic, and she faded into obscurity after World War II. But interest in her achievements was revived in 1972 by fashion designer Yves St. Laurent, who bought some of her work at auction. In 2009, Gray's "Dragons" armchair prototype (ca. 1919) sold for more than $28 million, setting a record for twentieth-century furniture that has yet to be surpassed.

The E1027 table (opposite), named after the seaside house she built in the south of France with her partner, Jean Badovici, is beautiful, functional, and affordable. This faithful reproduction is widely available now for around $99. It looks great, but the point is that it derives its form from its function: you can slide the base under your bed so that the glass top floats over your lap. The height can be adjusted via the attached key and notched chrome stem.

First impression: To quote the early-twentieth-century monologist Ruth Draper: "It's chrome and glass and steel. It's adorable."

! 5 ?

Expect delays.

This notice of a change (opposite) in New York subway service—printed on an 8½" x 11" sheet of paper and taped to a girder on the platform, ahem—isn't terrible, but it's not as clear as it could be, either. And it really needs to be clear. What they're doing here is compartmentalizing information, which sometimes works and sometimes doesn't. I'd say this is one of the times it doesn't.

On the next spread I've reworked the sign to be clearer, using the same language, proportions, and colors available.

First impression: What is happening, exactly, and when?

31

I have found that in cases like this, what is wanted is simple declarative sentences with a beginning, middle, and end, and which tell you directly what's going on.

What we see first (opposite) is that there's a service change (it doesn't matter whether it's "planned" or not), and then we see when it is happening and which train lines are affected. We keep the green circles around the white numbers, because that's how many people identify that particular train ("Just take the green line to City Hall, and then . . .").

It's also very important to include the Metropolitan Transportation Authority logo (which I think is great, by the way, because it implies forward movement) so that we know this is legit.

First impression: I will be taking the 5 train this weekend instead of the 4. On Monday it will be back to normal.

SERVICE CHANGE

THIS WEEKEND, APRIL 19-20

(3:30 AM SAT TO 10:00 PM SUN),

NO ④ TRAINS WILL BE RUNNING. TAKE THE ⑤ TRAIN INSTEAD.

⑤ TRAINS
REPLACE ④ TRAINS
IN MANHATTAN
AND BROOKLYN
DURING THIS TIME.

Counting down . . .

I am a habitually fast walker (because I'm always late, but that's another story), so when these crossing signals with countdown clocks started to appear at some Midtown Manhattan intersections in 2010, I was thrilled. They take all the guesswork out of deciding whether to try to beat the light or cool your heels at the curb.

It's not that the old system was bad, but this change makes a huge difference. Basically, when you see the white-lit walking figure (not pictured), it's okay to cross. Then, a red-lit hand appears next to the number twenty, which then counts down to zero (previously, there were no numbers). So, the image opposite (taken outside my apartment building) means that you now have twelve seconds left (and counting) to cross the street before you get run over. Or, stay put and wait for the walking man again. That's the kind of clarity I need.

Of course, *real* New Yorkers know that even when the countdown runs out you still have about five seconds to get across, but I probably shouldn't say that. Also, the "rule of physics" traffic law *always* applies to crossing the streets of New York City—that is, if there are no cars coming, go for it, regardless of what the light indicates. I shouldn't say that, either.

First impression: Twelve seconds to cross the street? An eternity. I can do that.

X marks the teeny, tiny, hard-to-find spot.

Don't you just love pop-up ads? Me, neither. And why would anyone, except adv[...]eed to rethink this, as far as I'm conce[...]ne ugly, intrusive, insulting, trying to[...]don't need or just flat-out lying, and [...] to get rid of. Most have a tiny x in the[...]that upon clicking will make them dis[...]get at especially on a smartphone. All t[...]gry at the sponsors and the websites th[...]r use them to buy anything.

But if effective [...]ves its goal, then I grudgingly have to [...]e effective and have achieved it, but the[...]r pissing people off. What kind of goal [...]as meant for better than this.

First impression: Intrusive design, diabolical purpose.

Picking up.

Even if I wasn't a Japanophile, I would still use chopsticks all the time, for all kinds of cuisine. Especially salads, which can be unwieldy on a fork. The cultural difference between selecting your food and stabbing it is symbolic of the quiet simplicity of the East versus the blunt directness of the West.

Chopsticks are a little tricky to master at first, but once you do, it can eventually seem a bit crude that you used to poke and prod at your meal with forks and knives. And chopsticks are great for noodle soups with ramen or udon, which spoons don't handle well.

This particular pair (opposite)—which I use to eat lunch at my desk—is made of resin, and thus is very washable and reusable, and doesn't absorb oils or other residue.

First impression: An elegant way to eat.

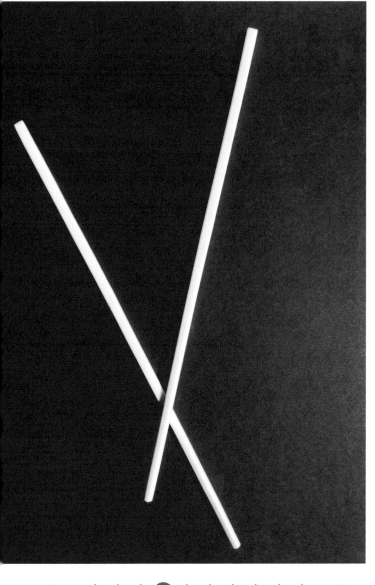

! 4 ?

Don't get me started.
Or do.

Now here is a mystery we just don't need, though it's one we have to face annually. Those of us who can afford to pay others to deal with it do so, and then deduct our accountant's fees from our incomes. That's more than a little crazy.

What makes taxes so maddening is the byzantine labyrinth of what's deductible and what isn't, and the fear that if you don't get the returns right, you will be audited. It's as though they're rigged from the start for you to fail, so you pay more than you need to just to be safe.

My first relationship was with a lovely Swiss fellow who was a banker, and he remarked that he didn't understand why the US tax system had to be so complicated.

"In Switzerland, they send us a tax bill that says how much we owe, and then we pay it. End of story."

That sounds so damned civilized.

First impression: You guys already know everything; can't you just tell me how much I owe?

Form 1040 Department of the Treasury—Internal Revenue Service (99)
U.S. Individual Income Tax Return **2013** OMB No. 1545-0074 IRS Use Only—Do not write or staple in this space.

For the year Jan. 1–Dec. 31, 2013, or other tax year beginning , 2013, ending , 20

See separate instructions.

Your first name and initial | Last name

Your social security number

If a joint return, spouse's first name and initial | Last name

Spouse's social security number

Home address (number and street). If you have a P.O. box, see instructions. | Apt. no.

▲ Make sure the SSN(s) above and on line 6c are correct.

City, town or post office, state, and ZIP code. If you have a foreign address, also complete spaces below (see instructions).

Presidential Election Campaign
Check here if you, or your spouse if filing jointly, want $3 to go to this fund. Checking a box below will not change your tax or refund. ☐ You ☐ Spouse

Foreign country name | Foreign province/state/county | Foreign postal code

Filing Status

Check only one box.

1 ☐ Single
2 ☐ Married filing jointly (even if only one had income)
3 ☐ Married filing separately. Enter spouse's SSN above and full name here. ▶
4 ☐ Head of household (with qualifying person). (See instructions.) If the qualifying person is a child but not your dependent, enter this child's name here. ▶
5 ☐ Qualifying widow(er) with dependent child

Exemptions

6a ☐ **Yourself.** If someone can claim you as a dependent, **do not** check box 6a . . .
b ☐ **Spouse** . . . .

Boxes checked on 6a and 6b

c **Dependents:**

(1) First name Last name	(2) Dependent's social security number	(3) Dependent's relationship to you	(4) ✓ if child under age 17 qualifying for child tax credit (see instructions)
			☐
			☐
			☐
			☐

If more than four dependents, see instructions and check here ▶ ☐

No. of children on 6c who:
• lived with you
• did not live with you due to divorce or separation (see instructions)

Dependents on 6c not entered above

Add numbers on lines above ▶

d Total number of exemptions claimed . . . .

Income

Attach Form(s) W-2 here. Also attach Forms W-2G and 1099-R if tax was withheld.

If you did not get a W-2, see instructions.

7 Wages, salaries, tips, etc. Attach Form(s) W-2 | 7
8a Taxable interest. Attach Schedule B if required | 8a
b Tax-exempt interest. **Do not** include on line 8a | 8b
9a Ordinary dividends. Attach Schedule B if required | 9a
b Qualified dividends | 9b
10 Taxable refunds, credits, or offsets of state and local income taxes | 10
11 Alimony received | 11
12 Business income or (loss). Attach Schedule C or C-EZ | 12
13 Capital gain or (loss). Attach Schedule D if required. If not required, check here ▶ ☐ | 13
14 Other gains or (losses). Attach Form 4797 | 14
15a IRA distributions | 15a | b Taxable amount | 15b
16a Pensions and annuities | 16a | b Taxable amount | 16b
17 Rental real estate, royalties, partnerships, S corporations, trusts, etc. Attach Schedule E | 17
18 Farm income or (loss). Attach Schedule F | 18
19 Unemployment compensation | 19
20a Social security benefits | 20a | b Taxable amount | 20b
21 Other income. List type and amount | 21
22 Combine the amounts in the far right column for lines 7 through 21. This is your **total income** ▶ | 22

Adjusted Gross Income

23 Educator expenses | 23
24 Certain business expenses of reservists, performing artists, and fee-basis government officials. Attach Form 2106 or 2106-EZ | 24
25 Health savings account deduction. Attach Form 8889 | 25
26 Moving expenses. Attach Form 3903 | 26
27 Deductible part of self-employment tax. Attach Schedule SE | 27
28 Self-employed SEP, SIMPLE, and qualified plans | 28
29 Self-employed health insurance deduction | 29
30 Penalty on early withdrawal of savings | 30
31a Alimony paid b Recipient's SSN ▶ | 31a
32 IRA deduction | 32
33 Student loan interest deduction | 33
34 Tuition and fees. Attach Form 8917 | 34
35 Domestic production activities deduction. Attach Form 8903 | 35
36 Add lines 23 through 35 | 36
37 Subtract line 36 from line 22. This is your **adjusted gross income** ▶ | 37

For Disclosure, Privacy Act, and Paperwork Reduction Act Notice, see separate instructions. Cat. No. 11320B Form **1040** (2013)

Where the toys are.

I love saving the heroes.

Ever since I can remember, I wanted to live in a comic-book museum when I grew up. I think I've pretty much achieved that. I've been collecting toys all my life, mostly of the vintage superhero variety; opposite is a photo of a wall in my apartment. I look at the toys every day, and what really inspires me beyond my fandom (which is huge, obviously) are the colors—the saturation and combination of the primaries: red, blue, and yellow (plus green, as in Lantern and Arrow). In a lot of my book-jacket designs I use variations on the primary colors, and I suspect this is why.

When you take the colors away from the costumes—as they have in the Batman movies since 1989, for example—it very much changes your perception of the characters. When Batman is all in black, it's not that it's not fun anymore, but it's a very different kind of fun. Ditto the X-Men. We seem to take them more seriously, which is kind of ridiculous and yet a fan's dream at the same time. Everything opposite is from 1966 or earlier, and includes a lot of toys from Japan. (I love the the pop-cultural cross-pollination.) The preservationist in me gets a charge out of the fact that none of this was meant to be saved in the package. These were created before toy collecting became a thing; they were meant to be consumed and ripped apart. They were never supposed to survive like this.

First impression: The basic is heroic.

! ┼──●──┼──┼──┼──┼──┼──┼── ?

2

Lead us not into Penn Station.

Certainly one of the most egregious New York design crimes of the last century was the destruction of the original Pennsylvania Station in 1962, and its replacement with the abysmal drop-ceilinged, overhead-fluorescent-lit, basement-level hell-pit under Madison Square Garden that remains today. It still somehow functions as the most-used transit hub in the United States, with more than 600,000 travelers moving in and out each day, at the rate of 1,000 people every 90 seconds. And yet it's an embarrassment of confusion and squalor, especially for a city that claims the mantle of Capital of the World (and yes, I use Penn Station all the time; I have to—I'm always on Amtrak).

In what appears to be a cruel joke, there are photos mounted on the gate pillars showing how spectacular the original vaulted Beaux Arts building used to be (opposite, bottom). Thanks a lot. But the mystery here is not only why it is so ugly, but how difficult it is to navigate through.

First impression: Airless, scuzzy, inefficient. A terrible introduction for visitors to New York City.

! ———————————————— ?

10

 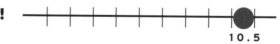

10.5

How refreshing.

This redesign of the Diet Coke can (opposite) is mysterious in the best possible way. Besides being formally striking, it assumes a level of intelligence and sophistication in its audience that is truly commendable, drawing on the "Less Is More" principles espoused by the architect Ludwig Mies van der Rohe. The visual vocabulary of the brand is reduced to its most essential parts, and we understand immediately what we're looking at, based on very little verbal information.

This is made possible by our decades-long familiarity with the logotype of the product and its application to a soda can. It's a cherished friend in fabulous new clothes, a BFF's makeover that you thought never could or would happen.

Truly great packaging.

First impression: Instantly recognizable; I don't even need to be able to read it. Thank you for trusting me.

Which makes the following advertising campaign all the more perplexing. Imagine that you are in the busy hub of the Times Square subway station, hurrying to catch your train, and you see this:

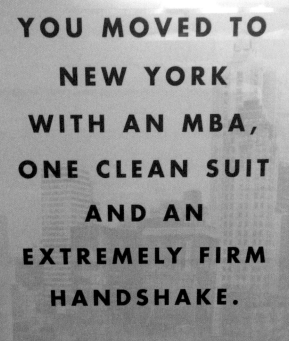

YOU MOVED TO
NEW YORK
WITH AN MBA,
ONE CLEAN SUIT
AND AN
EXTREMELY FIRM
HANDSHAKE.

YOU'RE ON.

Um . . .

The mystery here is not *what* are they saying, but *why* are they saying it?

These Diet Coke ads were, in contrast to the packaging, clear in the *worst* possible way. I would guess that whoever is responsible for this thought they were being naughty and cool, but as someone who has done design work for Coca-Cola in the past, I am baffled and amazed that this ever saw the light of day. Nothing like this can happen without a LOT of important people signing off on it.

And, to clarify, that is *not* a period after "YOU'RE ON"; it's a trademark symbol. Nice.

Excuse me— I'm on *what?*

! ●————————————— ?
1.5

Call me crazy, but if you're a corporation with the global reach and customer base of Coca-Cola, isn't it in your best interests to *not* liken the consumption of one of your most popular products to something as dangerous and potentially devastating as abusing illegal narcotics—to say nothing of your responsibilities to your consumers? Why did someone in a high place (sorry) think that this was a good idea? How do these decisions get made? The focus testing alone (which normally I hate) should have sealed these ads' fate, but it didn't.

Ironically, it was the public at large's reaction that killed the campaign. It was pulled in a matter of weeks, due to mass pushback via parodies of the ads that were tweeted and posted on YouTube.

And NO, I am NOT on coke. But I suspect there is an advertising executive somewhere who is. Ahem.

Now we'll move on to how additional everyday phenomena can influence things I actually have to make.

Let's look at . . .

Judgment
at work.

Okay, let's put our judgment to work. Here are some more examples of images and objects I see every day, but now I'll show how I've applied them to solving design problems in my working life (mostly involving book covers).

I've found it important to be constantly alive to the possibilities in my environment; that way, everything becomes fodder for ideas.

You never know when something might be useful, even if it's you . . .

Good morning.

I look at my tongue in the mirror every morning, and if it's not black, I'm good to go. If it *is* black, it usually means I had red wine the night before, and I brush it thoroughly. If I didn't have red wine, I call the doctor.

But seriously, a good look at your face in the morning can tell you all kinds of things: about your health, your mood, and how you will appear to everyone you meet for the rest of the day. Adjust accordingly.

You don't have to be a narcissist—you just have to pay a little attention.

First impression: There's a reason that your doctor tells you to say "Ahh." Learn what looking at your tongue can teach you about your well-being.

PROJECT:
GULP BY MARY ROACH
A BOOK ABOUT
THE HUMAN DIGESTIVE SYSTEM

Anyway, these sorts of things—mouths, health, and how we take in sustenance—were foremost on my mind when I was working on the cover of Mary Roach's book *Gulp*, her delightful and brilliant study of the human digestive system. The question was how to depict this and serve both the serious science involved and the witty spirit in which it was delivered.

There were many ways I could have gone about it, but the main thing I took away from reading the text was, how do I make the way the body digests food look *fun*? When I found this wonderful stock illustration from the Alamy agency, I knew it was perfect. Actual open mouths, as you have just seen, can be very off-putting in photographs. The witty spirit of this drawing gets us into the subject without putting us off.

In the end, I decided to start at the *beginning* of the digestive process, not . . . the end. Gulp.

Mary Roach

best-selling author of *Stiff*

Gulp.

ADVENTURES ALONG THE ALIMENTARY CANAL

! ——+——+——+——+——+——+——+——●——+—— ?
                                    8

Lather up.

They don't make things like they used to, especially when it comes to grooming products. I bought this 1940s-era single-blade razor at a flea market nearly twenty-five years ago. It sits on my bathroom shelf, and I use it regularly. I love the considerable heft of it, and how it feels in my hand: sturdy, strong, capable. Plus, there's a large spring in the core, so when you wind up the base and let go, it vibrates, combining the idea of an electric razor with the more effective practicality of a manual. Works great, looks beautiful.

First impression: Great industrial design is not disposable.

59

60

NICOLE KIDMAN
ROBERT DOWNEY JR.
FROM THE DIRECTOR OF *SECRETARY*

A FILM BY STEVEN SHAINBERG

F U R

AN IMAGINARY PORTRAIT OF DIANE ARBUS

! |———|———|———|———|———|———|———|———●——— ?

10

Film director Steven Shainberg asked me to create the teaser campaign for *Fur*, his truly kooky but fascinating biopic about the genius photographer Diane Arbus. The project was totally opposed by Arbus's estate, so none of her pictures could be used, either on the poster or in the movie itself. But Shainberg made the film anyway, with Nicole Kidman and Robert Downey Jr., in what has to be one of the least successful movies with an A-list cast in recent memory. In it, Downey plays a circus-freak wolfman-figure with a body totally covered in hair, and in a climactic scene Kidman's Arbus takes a razor (not unlike my vintage model) and shaves every square inch of it off. I thought the connection be- tween the stark visual of the razor juxtaposed with the clipped verbal title would make an interesting tease (photos of the stars were used in the main campaign that followed this), while promi- nently featuring the names of the actors would assure viewers that this was a film to take notice of. Alas, not that many people did.

61

Get your balance.

Do you remember when you used to actually have to go to the bank teller to get money? Probably not.

Automated teller machines became popular in the late 1970s and were a revelation of convenience. But there were two problems: 1) they literally swallowed your bank card in order to read it, and sometimes didn't give it back; and 2) the keypad for entering your PIN was often conspicuously placed, giving cyber-pickpocketing Peeping Toms too much ammunition.

That has changed, for the better. This machine (opposite) near my office is typical of most, in that the card reader scans the card without making it disappear. The addition of touch-screens and security cameras (upper left) have made sidewalk banking not only safe but the norm. Headphone jacks for the hearing impaired and braille on the keys—followed by audio instructions for the blind—certainly help those who would otherwise be unable to use ATMs. Yes, banking apps for smartphones are great, but as long as we need cash (and we will always need cash; sorry, Bitcoin peeps and Apple Pay), these machines are the way to go.

First impression: I push a button and money comes out. It's like magic! And secure and safe—a beautiful thing.

THIS ATM OFFERS AUDIO
ASSISTANCE FOR THE
VISUALLY IMPAIRED.

63

Beth Kobliner (a dear friend) is sort of the Suze Orman for people who want straightforward personal financial planning information without a lot flash and fanfare, and she asked me to do the cover for her book about money management for young people. An ATM receipt definitely seemed to be the answer. But what you're seeing instead of your bank balance is what you should be doing *with* it.

64

This is called appropriating the visual vernacular, which means using a visual trope or conceit having to do with one kind of information and applying it to another. See also *The Mind's Eye*, page 80, and *Brazzaville Beach*, page 96.

THE NEW YORK TIMES BESTSELLER

GET A FINANCIAL LIFE

PERSONAL FINANCE
IN YOUR TWENTIES
AND THIRTIES

GET OUT OF DEBT
AFFORD A HOME OF YOUR OWN
INVEST WISELY WITH LITTLE MONEY
IMPROVE YOUR CREDIT SCORE
PAY LESS IN TAXES

BETH KOBLINER

How much?

The clarity of the design of the dollar bill has been consistently effective for more than one hundred and fifty years, no matter how it has varied: the image of George Washington is just perfect as the representation of the birth of the United States and its currency: he can be trusted, relied on, and believed in (he can't tell a lie!).

The two green tones (soothing, reassuring, earthy), the precise engraving and stamping, the texture of the resilient cotton and linen paper in the hand that can withstand countless transactions—this is great graphic design that hundreds of millions of people interact with every day.

First impression: In this we trust.

THE AMERICAN PEOPLE BY LARRY KRAMER

A NOVEL ABOUT
THE HISTORY OF THE UNITED STATES

Larry Kramer's searing fictional revisionist history of the United States includes a panoply of well-known figures, including George Washington, Abraham Lincoln, Malcolm X, Martin Luther King Jr., and many more. I chose to start at the beginning, with Washington, and take a detail of a famous portrait of him from 1796 by Gilbert Stuart. I was definitely influenced by the dollar bill, but I thought that by actually using that, this would look too much like a book about finance, which it definitely is not.

Even though the close-up is extreme, we know Washington's face so well that, coupled with the book's title, the viewer can easily put two and two together: this is going to be a new point of view on the American Story. The boldness and modernity of the typeface (Blender by Nik Thoenen) signals that this is a contemporary take on historical material.

THE AMERICAN PEOPLE

VOLUME 1: SEARCH FOR MY HEART

LARRY KRAMER

! —+—+—+—+—+—+—●—+— ?

9

Like five fingers.

When designing the cover of a book, one starts with the text and uses it as a guide to suggest visuals. In my case, since I mostly work on hardcover first editions, the text is usually in the form of an unedited manuscript. There is something about reading a book in its raw form that helps me really get into the head of the author; I feel like I am there at the creation of the work.

In Haruki Murakami's *Colorless Tsukuru Tazaki and His Years of Pilgrimage*, there was a particular phrase about a third of the way in that seemed to define what the jacket should be. The story itself is about the title character's sudden exile from his four very closest friends' circle, for no apparent reason, and his long journey back from the pit of despair this plunges him into. It takes years for him to heal from this, and then to gain the courage to confront his friends one by one to find out why they cast him out. In the meantime he becomes fascinated by the Tokyo transit system and eventually finds meaningful employment as an engineer designing train stations.

The first of the friends he tracks down is Ao, who now has a successful Lexus dealership in their hometown of Nagoya. He seems to have no animosity toward Tsukuru, and when they go to lunch and talk, he recalls the five friends in the manner you see underlined in red on the opposite page.

First impression: An image of a hand is the perfect metaphor to depict the closeness of this quintet.

ole

"I don't g

ess background.
person was necessary
ou weren't empty.
rest of us relax."

...?" Tsukuru repeated, surprised. "Like

that. It's hard to explain, but having you there, we
n't say much, but you had your feet solidly planted on the
up a sense of security. Like an anchor. We saw that more clear
ith us anymore. How much we really needed you. I don't know if tha
after you left, we all sort of went our separate ways."

sukuru remained silent, unable to find the right reply.

"You know, in a sense we were a perfect combination, the five of us. Like five
." Ao raised his right hand and spread his thick fingers. "I still think that. The five
ers: us all naturally made up for what was lacking in the others, and totally shared our
better qualities. I doubt that sort of thing will ever happen again in our lives. It was a on
time occurrence. I have my own family now, and of course I love them. But truthfully
don't have the same spontaneous, pure feeling for them that I had for all of you bac
n."

Tsukuru was silent. Ao crushed the empty paper bag into a ball and rol
his large hand.

uru, I believe you," Ao said. "That you didn't do anything to
makes perfect sense. You'd never do something like th
was wondering how to respond, *Viva Las Vegas!*
cked the caller's name and stuffed the ph

**COLORLESS TSUKURU TAZAKI AND HIS YEARS
OF PILGRIMAGE
BY HARUKI MURAKAMI**

A NOVEL ABOUT

FOUR CLOSE FRIENDS WHO CAST OUT A FIFTH

The image of a hand here is abstracted, and may not be clear at first. That is fine, because a major theme in the story is that Tsukuru's banishment is a total mystery to him. His four friends—two men, two women—have names that in Japanese correspond to colors: Mr. Red, Mr. Blue, Miss White, and Miss Black. Tsukuru's name has no such association, so he goes by Colorless. He is represented here as the "thumb" on the hand—a symbolic anchor that supports the others—and is represented by a detail of a Tokyo railway map, which just happens to use the colors of his friends.

Note that when Ao makes the reference to five fingers (page 71), he raises his right hand, so that determined which hand I should depict.

On the physical book, each of the five "fingers" is actually a die-cut window (literally, a hole punched out by the printer with a metal die) in the jacket itself, and when you remove it, the visual narrative on the cover/binding continues and leads to a new meaning.

This design is not meant to be immediately understood; the idea is to entice the reader to investigate the book in order to decode it. But the materials used—silver ink for the background, cellophane behind each finger-window—are very clearly intended to draw you in, in a way that an image on a screen (or even on the opposite page) cannot.

COLORLESS TSUKURU TAZAKI

AND HIS YEARS OF PILGRIMAGE

A NOVEL

HARUKI MURAKAMI

! 8 ?

I'll have . . .

I didn't know what carrot cake was until I came to New York and saw the thick and creamy slices under the city's famed delicatessen counters. I was dubious: making a cake out of carrots seemed about as good a plan as making ice cream out of zucchini (which someone, somewhere, has no doubt done by now—probably in Brooklyn).

And yet one bite proved it delicious, mainly because it was so bolstered by slabs of buttercream icing, sugar, and lots of spices that the carrots themselves really became a gastric afterthought.

But what really got me design-wise was the orange-and-green confectioner's decoration in the shape of a carrot on the top of each piece, to remind you of the "main" ingredient. This illusion—the implication that a product is good for you because it's made out of something that's good for you—has been used in advertising for years, for products such as Land O'Lakes butter, menthol cigarettes, Apple Jacks cereal, and raspberry Pop Tarts.

Caveat emptor.

First impression: It's got to be healthful—look at the little carrot on top of it!

!   5   ?

And so I was faced with creating an image for former surgeon general David Kessler's book on how to deal with the rise of obesity in this country.

The original title was going to be *Sugar, Salt, Fat*, which would have been much, much easier to deal with, because it's very direct and would have contrasted brilliantly with images of anonymous overweight people from the, um, rear.

But then David decided he wanted the book to be not just about the problem of obesity but also what can be done to help solve it. Thus *The End of Overeating*.

76

Okay, fine, but how do you *show* that? Do you have people sitting at tables with empty plates in front of them, not eating? Such an image wouldn't get the point across. That's when I harkened back to the carrot cake and its origins. This scheme (opposite) can be perceived as Before and After, going from top to bottom: so you see the cake first, get scolded/informed, and then see what you really should be eating.

The book was number one on the *New York Times* bestseller list for several weeks, and Kessler remarked to me on more than one occasion afterward that it was because of the icing.

Fine, I thought; as long as you can only look at it.

The end of overeating.

CONTROLLING THE
INSATIABLE AMERICAN APPETITE

DAVID A. KESSLER, M. D.

! 8.5 ?

Can you read
the top line?

Eye charts—developed in the mid-nineteenth century by Dr. Franciscus Donders and his colleague Herman Snellen in the Netherlands—fascinate me because they are meant to be read, but not in any conventional sense (out loud, without conveying coherent meaning). They start out extremely clearly at the top, and then get more mysterious line by line, depending on your eyesight.

Form and content are completely divorced from each other here, because if the letters spelled out actual words, it would be easier to cheat at reading what they are. Most examples, like this one (opposite), use serifs on the letters—the extra lines on the ends—to render them harder to make out as they get smaller.

This is a simple, inexpensive, and low-tech solution that has become visually iconic and is still in use after one hundred and fifty years.

First impression: E! Now how low can I go?

$\frac{20}{200}$	**E**	200 FT. 61 m
$\frac{20}{100}$	**F P**	100 FT. 30.5 m
$\frac{20}{75}$	**T O Z**	70 FT. 21.3 m
$\frac{20}{50}$	**L P E D**	50 FT. 15.2 m
$\frac{20}{40}$	**P E C F D**	40 FT. 12.2 m
$\frac{20}{30}$	**E D F C Z P**	30 FT. 9.14 m
$\frac{20}{25}$	**F E L O P Z D**	25 FT. 7.62 m
$\frac{20}{20}$	**D E F P O T E C**	20 FT. 6.10 m
$\frac{20}{15}$	L E F O D P C T	15 FT. 4.57 m
$\frac{20}{13}$	F D P L T C E O	13 FT. 3.96 m
$\frac{20}{10}$	P E Z O L C F T D	10 FT. 3.05 m

79

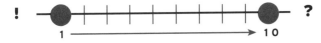

So the famed neurologist and writer Oliver Sacks goes to the eye doctor for his annual checkup, and the letters on the eye chart start to do funny things. Thus begins his exploration of visual perception in the brain, along with an investigation into the cases of six other extraordinary people who have learned to cope with extreme and often potentially devastating changes in their vision.

The visual vernacular here of an eye chart was a no-brainer (sorry), but what makes this different is the letterforms going in and out of focus to mimic Sacks's experience. On a book cover, something like this has to be handled very carefully so that it remains readable.

And then there is the color. My original design was much more muted, skewing to the generally monochromatic nature of the source material, but Oliver wanted something livelier, because the stories are actually about overcoming adversity. He was right: the iconography of an eye chart is so recognizable that it can easily withstand being rendered in bright red and yellow.

And its calling attention to itself on the bookshelf didn't hurt, to say the least.

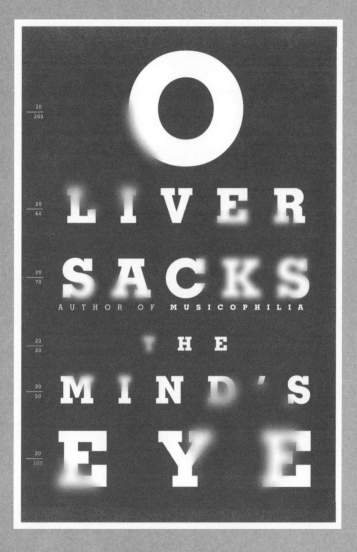

Say what? Say *that*.

As a resident of New York City over the past several decades, and one who creates visuals for a living, I have truly mixed feelings about graffiti. By definition it's a marring of public property, and if it goes unchecked around me, it makes me feel that anarchy has taken over. This is not a good thing, trust me (East Berlin, anyone?). Also, the messages are usually indecipherable and ultimately drown each other out.

Then there's a whole other kind of graffiti—which I see mostly on advertising posters in the subway—that sometimes really *does* have something to say, and to me is far more interesting. In this particular case (opposite), it is commentary on the apartment-sharing phenomenon of Airbnb (please note: I am not expressing my opinion of Airbnb, I am just commenting on someone else's viewpoint).

We are told clearly that this person is against this service, but it leads to questions as to why (bedbugs? Really?). Still, this is a strong statement that is communicated directly and plainly, and leaves the viewer with something to think about beyond what the sponsor intended.

Often these kinds of "annotations" are puerile and vulgar, but this one isn't. Someone really cares about the issue and wants to inform the public. It's now up to you to investigate it, if you want to, and draw your own conclusions.

First impression: Freedom of expression here is not limited to print advertisers by any means. Anyone with a Magic Marker and a reaction can chime in, too.

So for David Rakoff's book of essays, *Fraud*, I decided to apply this "annotation" concept as well.

Most of the pieces in this book involve assignments the urbanite author had taken that he was not qualified to do: white-water rafting down the Colorado River; climbing an icy mountain in cheap loafers; and, perhaps most memorably, impersonating Sigmund Freud in a Barneys department store window during the Christmas holiday season. All of these dubious forays add up to the conclusion that Rakoff was misrepresenting himself.

So my idea was that you've bought the new book by David Rakoff (no other typography on the jacket), and as you start to read you begin to suspect you've been hoodwinked: this guy isn't who he says he is. So out of frustration you take a big red Magic Marker and scribble "FRAUD" on the jacket. This implies a catharsis, and looks pretty good and spontaneous, too. In the printing process of this jacket, it was all too easy to mimic the subtle texture of an actual red squeaky pen.

It was fun to see rows of these on bookstore shelves, looking as if some nut had sneaked in after hours and scrawled all over them.

FRAUD

David Rakoff

Where am I?

Google Earth is truly a marvel as an exploration tool (and Superman-flight-simulator), but it has also caused some controversy regarding privacy rights: just how much surveillance should be at everyone's fingertips? This will be an ongoing conversation, of course, but I think what would truly change the game is if Google Earth enabled you to see everything going on in real time. And it doesn't: this most recent overhead shot of my apartment block (opposite, in the middle) is more than three years old. I know that because the progress on the decades-in-the-making Second Avenue subway line is much further along than what I see here (thank god!). So in that sense Google Earth is literally the world's largest still photograph of the planet, which makes it much more of a map resource than a spy tool. The key to keeping it relevant will lie in constantly updating it.

I like it when newscasters report on something going on in a place that I'm not geographically familiar with. The camera usually starts out in a wide angle, high above the outline of a country or state, and then starts to descend, picking up speed, and zoom—you're there, and have gotten specifically oriented to where the activity is in less than three seconds.

But what Google Earth does best, and quite beautifully, is lend perspective. Look at how small we are, how close we are to our neighbors, how intricately our surroundings are structured. This, of course, is more pronounced in highly populated areas. What are the implications?

First impression: I better understand my environment when I can look at it from a new angle.

87

! ●————|————|————|————|————|————|————|————|————|———— ?
  1

For the cover of Alan Ehrenhalt's study of the revitalization of urban environments, it seemed only natural to put Google Earth images to use (with permission, of course).

So opposite is Bushwick, Brooklyn, which is one of the author's case studies about the renewed desire to move from the suburbs back to cities and reclaim formerly desolate downtown areas.

But from this height, the photo could be of any of a host of places in America, and that serves Ehrenhalt's thesis that this phenomenon of reurbanization is happening all over the country. The gridded texture of city blocks simultaneously suggests the idea of complexity and order, two of the major themes of the book.

THE GREAT INVERSION

AND THE FUTURE OF THE AMERICAN CITY

ALAN EHRENHALT

CMYK

As a working print designer, I had to learn very early on about the offset lithography process (also called four-color printing) and how it works. Basically, all full-color images are composed of combinations of four components: cyan (blue), magenta (a pinkish red), yellow, and black (referred to by printers as K so as not be confused with blue). White is taken care of by the color of the paper itself. If you have a personal printer at home, then you know that there are four ink cartridges containing these colors inside, and the black one usually runs out first, because it's used in just about everything.

These colors are broken down into dot patterns called halftone screens, and when combined in the right ways, they can make just about any other color you can imagine (except fluorescents or metallics; they require their own special inks).

First impression: A brilliant system—from four simple building blocks, you can create millions of options.

YELLOW MAGENTA CYAN   BLACK

91

! ⊢—┼—┼—┼—┼—┼—●—┼—┼—┼—┼—┤ ?
                    6

LOGOTYPE FOR ABRAMS COMICARTS

Four-color printing has always been used to make comic books, and when the Abrams publishing house announced they were going to start a division that specialized in graphic novels (a fancy name for comic books), they asked me to create a logotype to give them a distinct visual identity.

92

The word "logo" is derived from the ancient Greek for "word," and refers to a graphic symbol that is used to identify and promote an organization (usually a commercial concern) or individual. The term "logotype" differs slightly from "logo" because it depicts the actual name of what it represents.

The solution for Abrams ComicArts was to be found in the components of the printing process itself. What do you see here?

The use of color enables the viewer to perceive this mark in four different ways: "Abrams ComicArts," "Abrams Art," "Comics," and "Art." Not unlike CMYK.

! —+—+—+—+—+—+—●—+—+—+— ?

Smoked.

I have never smoked, but as much as I hate commercial tobacco, I do admit I admire many cigarette package designs because so many use what I call "separation of type and state," or the civilized division of typography and image. This is a separation (or distinction, if you will) that I make as someone who appreciates visual dichotomy: the aesthetic distance from what something looks like and what it represents.

This design (opposite) even holds up when it's crushed and stomped into the street, because the typography is classic, the colors are pure, and the proportions are balanced.

First impression: Filthy habit, clean design. Even when it's filthy.

BRAZZAVILLE BEACH **BY WILLIAM BOYD**
A NOVEL ABOUT A SCIENTIST IN AFRICA

In this story about a Jane Goodall–like researcher of primates in Africa, the main character smokes an obscure local brand of cigarettes called Tuskers. They don't actually exist, but other African brands certainly do, so I visited smoke shops around the neighborhood of the United Nations building in New York to see what the packaging of these brands looked like (this was before the Internet existed). I borrowed several elements from them to make this cover: warm colors, linear geometry, an airplane, retro lettering, and gold foil across the top. The small strip of mathematical symbols over the plane is a reference to the main character's husband's job as a numerical theoretician (which eventually drives him mad).

Even if the source material is not initially recognizable, I am hoping that it doesn't matter to the reader so long as it piques his or her interest.

BRAZZAVILLE
beach

A NOVEL

WILLIAM BOYD

AUTHOR OF

A GOOD MAN IN AFRICA & AN ICE-CREAM WAR

Have we Met?

Who needs Chippendale's when you can go to the Metropolitan Museum? I'm kidding! Sort of. Well, not really. But certainly the ancient Roman and Greek statuary galleries there contain some of the most extraordinary examples of stone carving in the world. And they are indeed sensual.

A sculptor friend of mine once put it succinctly: How do you make a block of marble look like it's actually breathing? The question is as simple and as complex as that, and the answer lies in techniques that I can't begin to understand but at which I endlessly marvel. That the artists usually choose to depict idealized physical specimens (gods, goddesses, nymphs, satyrs, etc.) only makes the end product all the more enticing. They were the supermodels of their day. Did anyone really want to see a statue depicting imperfection? Back then, what would be the point?

But then there are the fragments of the figures that didn't survive the ages, which leave us to imagine the rest of them. These elicit a different kind of fascination because of what's missing and our desire to fill in the blanks to complete them.

Would the Venus de Milo be nearly as interesting with her arms intact? I think most people would say no (and yes, I know that's the Louvre—just saying).

First impression: Looks like flesh, yet hard as a rock. How did they *do* that? What was the process?

! 1 0 ?

101

How do you encapsulate the idea of a contemporary (and, sadly, now deceased) historian and renowned art critic expounding upon one of the greatest ancient cities of the Western world? Well, I thought a statue fragment wouldn't be the worst way to go, especially given the special limitations on the front of the jacket (large, iconic title, ditto author name; not a lot of room left for the image). An entire head would have taken up too much space, and what's really important here is the idea of storytelling—oral tradition passed down from generation to generation.

So, talk to me, Professor Hughes. Tell me all about it.

102

ROME

A CULTURAL, VISUAL, AND PERSONAL HISTORY

ROBERT
HUGHES

Jolly Roger.

I'm not sure when skulls and crossbones started to appear as a motif on clothing and accessories, but it's been happening for years now, and there's a timelessness to the symbol that is endearing, classic, and kind of horrifying, when you really think about it.

The skull-and-bones pirate flag originated in the 1700s and was flown on invading ships only when they came within firing range of the legitimate commercial vessels they sought to capture. The idea was to give their targets an opportunity to surrender without a fight. If they didn't, the black flags went down and were replaced with red ones—and all the implications that went along with them.

So the black pirate flags were, in the relative scheme of things, meant to be peaceful in a way: submit, and no one gets hurt.

That's a mantra, I'd say, that isn't at all irrelevant to the fashion business.

First impression: Yo ho ho and an embroidered belt!

! 10 ?

PROJECT:
VILLAIN
BY SHUICHI YOSHIDA
A NOVEL ABOUT A MURDER IN JAPAN

In photographer Francois Robert's Stop The Violence series, bones are ingeniously arrranged to create images of weaponry. "I use the human skeleton as the formal visual element, the subject of the image," he says. "In this manner, the skeleton is both the protagonist and antagonist (the Buddhist notion about "the duality of man"* seems apt). I intend the images to plant the notion of restraint and charity in an effort to promote peace and tolerance."

I had admired Robert's work for a long time, and when I received a manuscript for a novel called *Villain* by Shuichi Yoshida about the killing of a young woman in Japan, the two artistic sensibilities—of the photographer and the writer—seemed to go together.

This is a big part of what an art director does—gives form to a received piece of content. It's kind of like aesthetic matchmaking, pairing up the verbal with an arresting (so to speak, in this case) visual.

* Can be interpreted as the duality of one's state of consciousness and one's physical being. In Chinese philosophy this is the yin and the yang.

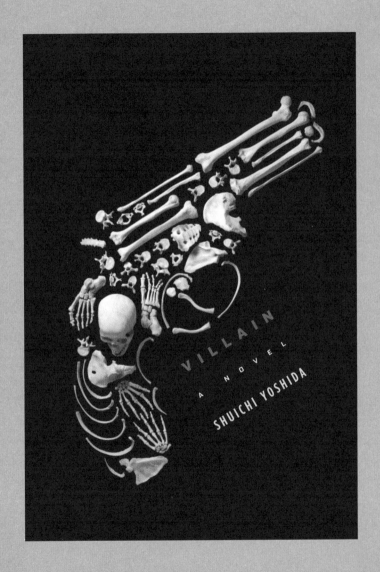

VILLAIN

A NOVEL

SHUICHI YOSHIDA

Good-bye.

I push this button (opposite) at the end of every workday in order to open the glass doors to the elevator vestibule on my floor of our office building so I can leave. The button is very clearly marked, but the mystery is why it exists in the first place. It's obviously another security measure, but what is it securing against? My leaving? Why?

There are red buttons to push all over New York City, usually in case of emergency: in elevators, on subway platforms, in street corner call boxes. But this isn't one of those; it's simply to open a door and let me out.

First impression: What is the danger here?

PROJECT:
PERFIDIA BY JAMES ELLROY
A NOVEL ABOUT THE EFFECT
OF PEARL HARBOR ON LOS ANGELES

The red button becomes something else entirely in this design for James Ellroy's book about what the events of December 7, 1941, mean to the City of Angels, and the way a horrific crime being investigated by detective/chemist Hideo Ashida of the LAPD somehow relates to all of it. The internment of his fellow Japanese-Americans in California at the dawn of the US involvement in World War II only exacerbates the tension, anxiety, and fear.

I tried to mimic that tension visually on this cover by pairing the graphically striking Japanese flag, the "rising sun," with the instantly recognizable nighttime grid of the streets of Los Angeles. This creates a visual standoff of light and dark, close-up and long view, bright and moody.

The idea here is that even if you don't know what "perfidia" means, you will want to find out.

JAMES ELLROY

PERFIDIA

A NOVEL

! —+—+—+—+—+—+—+—+—●—+— ?

9.5

Fender bender.

You never know what you'll see in the gutters of New York City, and when I came upon this (opposite) while walking to the subway one morning, I couldn't help but try to decode the story: a yellow taxi hit another car, or vice versa, and this was the residue. It was not as if I was at the scene of the accident—the source of it was long gone, or otherwise not in evidence.

But the conclusions to be drawn from the colors, the materials, the shattered bits, were undeniable. I've lived in the city long enough to know that insurance numbers were definitely exchanged.

Move along, people, nothing more to see here.

First impression: Small fragments can tell much larger stories.

113

8

Fiction writer Jay McInerney chronicles the high lives and low points of New York's demimonde, and a perfect source of imagery to illustrate this is brilliant society photographer Patrick McMullan. He took both of these pictures (opposite), and look how different they are: from the fashion-show runway excitement of the night before (top) to the sobering taxi-wreck reality of the morning after (bottom).

114

In contrasting these two sensibilities—night and day, happy and sad, delirious and slapped-to-attention—I tried to emphasize the wake-up call that the author brings to his readers.

And the pretty colors are nice, too.

Jay McInerney

NEW AND COLLECTED STORIES

HOW IT ENDED

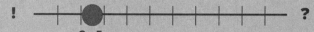

! ————|—●—|—|—|—|—|—|—|— ?

2.5

What's going to happen next?

Well, that's one of the biggest mysteries of all, isn't it? Fortune cookies have been around for the past hundred years, and we hold out hope, after a Chinese meal, that they will tell us what to expect. Or at least we are entertained by them, spurred on to think about what they might mean. On the one hand, it's silly; on the other, it's possibly something to think about.

The design of the fortunes is a fascinating combination of simplicity and reduction that enlivens the theater of the mind and its infinite conjectures on the possibilities of fate. And all from one sentence on a tiny slip of paper!

And then, of course, there's interpretation: the fortunes are deliberately vague, so that we draw from our personal experiences in order to bring an explanation to them.

First impression: What does this mean, and how does it apply to me?

Hardly anyone knows how much is gained by ignoring the future.

! ┼─┼─┼─┼─┼─┼─┼─┼─┼─┼─┼ ?

ALL THE BEAUTY YOU WILL EVER NEED
BY DAVID SEDARIS

AN ESSAY COLLECTION

This was the book that eventually became *When You Are Engulfed in Flames*, and it is the only jacket in this volume that didn't actually get produced. As sometimes happens in publishing, the author was weighing several different titles, and finally selected a different one.

Such a change also, of course, affects the cover design process and how I adapt my methods. The original title, *All the Beauty You Will Ever Need*, didn't directly apply to the content of any of the essays in the book, so in that sense I was free to think about an original context for the phrase. A Chinese fortune cookie seemed apt, as it provided a visual that I thought most everyone could recognize, yet had an attending sense of mystery. Note that the form of the slip of paper is so strong and recognizable that I didn't need to include cracked bits of cookie around it.

118

When the final title became what it is, I tried using it with the same design scheme, but it just didn't work—I think mainly because fortune cookies never tell you anything as shocking as the fact that you're on fire, right now.

David found a painting by van Gogh of a skeleton smoking, and that was great—the subject had already been through it all.

And so, yet again . . .

Clarity
gets to
the
point.

I find that the older I get (I turned fifty during the making of this book), the clearer I want things to be. I think this is a natural symptom of maturation—as we age, mysteries pile up, and they're usually not the fun ones:

Just how long do I have?

Why do some people get what they deserve, and others don't?

Why are certain problems so easy to solve, while others are totally impossible?

Will they ever, ever bring working jetpacks to the market-place?

Whoever you are, whatever you do for a living, you have problems to solve. I hope that this book has given you a little something to think about in terms of how you might proceed to do so. Ask yourself: What is this problem I'm trying to solve? How do I define it? What are its components? What is the goal I'm trying to achieve with its solution?

And remember . . .

Mystery gives us hope.

As we go on, Mystery becomes more important, too, because it helps us deal with things we can't understand.

It is fueled by faith: belief in ourselves, our friends, "the system," humanity in general, and whatever else it is we need to believe in. There's a reason we don't want great magic tricks explained.

Mystery is also valuable as a coping mechanism—the things that are all too clear are piling up, too:

Life is short.

Love can't be taken for granted.

Everything has a cost.

Just holding on to something doesn't mean it won't go away.

You can try to solve everything, but if you can't, that's okay. As long as you've tried your best.

And . . .

Always try to leave a good lasting impression.

So: what's clear to you?

And what isn't?

Those are not unimportant questions. Ditto these:

Are you clear to others when you need to be?

Do you understand how to use clarity and mystery, and when each is necessary?

Do you pay attention to how you are perceived by the world, no matter how big or small that world is?

Which brings us back to first impressions, a fitting way to end this little meditation. With this book, I've underscored the importance of healthy judgment. But I've also tried to introduce you to a few ideas (via my ideas, I am well aware) that might encourage you to look at things a little differently than you used to.

Did I succeed?

You be the judge . . .

Thank you:

Michelle Quint,

June Cohen,

Susan Lehman,

Gina Barnett,

Geoff Spear,

J. D. McClatchy,

Chee Pearlman,

David Rockwell,

Chris Anderson.

ABOUT THE AUTHOR

CHIP KIDD is a designer and writer living in New York City. His book cover designs for Alfred A. Knopf, where he has worked nonstop since 1986, have helped create a revolution in the art of American book packaging. He is the recipient of the National Design Award for Communication Design, as well as the Use of Photography in Design Award from the International Center of Photography. Kidd has published two novels, *The Cheese Monkeys* and *The Learners*. A distinguished and prolific lecturer, Kidd has spoken at Princeton, Yale, Harvard, RISD, and a zillion other places.

WATCH CHIP KIDD'S TED TALK

Chip Kidd's TED Talk, now available for free at TED.com, is the companion to *Judge This*.

JAMES DUNCAN DAVIDSON/TED

Yves Béhar: *Designing Objects That Tell Stories*

Designer Yves Béhar digs up his creative roots to discuss some of the iconic objects he's created (the Leaf lamp, the Jawbone headset). Then he turns to the witty, surprising, elegant objects he's working on now—including the $100 laptop.

John Hodgman: *Design, Explained*

John Hodgman, comedian and resident expert, "explains" the design of three iconic modern objects.

John Maeda: *Designing Simplicity*

The MIT Media Lab's John Maeda lives at the intersection of technology and art, a place that can get very complicated. Here he talks about paring down to basics.

Stefan Sagmeister: *Happiness by Design*

Graphic designer Stefan Sagmeister takes the audience on a whimsical journey through moments of his life that made him happy—and notes how many of these moments have to do with good design.

TED Books are small books about big ideas. They're short enough to read in a single sitting, but long enough to delve deep into a topic. The wide-ranging series covers everything from architecture to business, space travel to love, and is perfect for anyone with a curious mind and an expansive love of learning.

Each TED Book is paired with a related TED Talk, available online at TED .com. The books pick up where the talks leave off. An 18-minute speech can plant a seed or spark the imagination, but many talks create a need to go deeper, to learn more, to tell a longer story. TED Books fill this need.

ALSO FROM TED BOOKS

The Future of Architecture in 100 Buildings
by Marc Kushner

We're entering a new age in architecture—one where we expect our buildings to deliver far more than just shelter. Filled with gorgeous imagery and witty insight, this book is an essential guide to the future being built around us—a future that matters more, and to more of us, than ever.

THE
FUTURE
OF
ARCHITECTURE
IN
100
BUILDINGS

BY
MARC KUSHNER

EDITED BY JENNIFER KRICHELS

TED Books
Simon & Schuster

New York   London   Toronto   Sydney   New Delhi

TEDBooks

Simon & Schuster, Inc.
1230 Avenue of the Americas
New York, NY 1002
Copyright © 2015 by Marc Kushner

TED, the TED logo, and TED Books are trademarks
of TED Conferences, LLC.

First TED Books hardcover edition March 2015

TED BOOKS and colophon are registered trademarks
of TED Conferences, LLC

SIMON & SCHUSTER and colophon are registered trademarks
of Simon & Schuster, Inc.

For information about special discounts for bulk purchases,
please contact Simon & Schuster Special Sales at 1-866-506-1949
or business@simonandschuster.com.

For information on licensing the TED Talk that accompanies
this book, or other content partnerships with TED,
please contact TEDBooks@TED.com.

Cover and interior design by: MGMT. design
Series design by: Chip Kidd
Cover photo by David Frank

Manufactured in the United States of America

10   9   8   7   6   5   4   3

Library of Congress Cataloging-in-Publication Data is available.

ISBN 978-1-4767-8492-2
ISBN 978-1-4767-8493-9 (ebook)

TED is a nonprofit devoted to spreading ideas, usually in the form of short, powerful talks (eighteen minutes or less). TED began in 1984 as a conference where Technology, Entertainment, and Design converged, and today covers almost all topics—from science to business to global issues—in more than one hundred languages. Meanwhile, independently run TEDx events help share ideas in communities around the world.

TED is a global community, welcoming people from every discipline and culture who seek a deeper understanding of the world. We believe passionately in the power of ideas to change attitudes, lives, and, ultimately, the world. On TED.com, we're building a clearinghouse of free knowledge from the world's most inspired thinkers—and a community of curious souls to engage with ideas and each other, both online and at TED and TEDx events around the world, all year long.

In fact, everything we do—from our TED Talks videos to the projects sparked by the TED Prize, from the global TEDx community to the TED-Ed lesson series—is driven by this goal: How can we best spread great ideas?

TED is owned by a nonprofit, nonpartisan foundation.

EXTREME LOCATIONS

REINVENTION

GET BETTER

CONTENTS

POP-UP

SHAPE-SHIFTERS

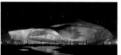

DRIVE

CONTENTS

THE
FUTURE
OF
ARCHITECTURE
IN
100
BUILDINGS

Introduction

This book wants you to ask more from architecture.

You live in a house, you work in an office, you send your kids to a school. These places aren't just the backdrop to your life, they shape your life—they define who you see, what you see, and how you see it.

Architecture impacts how you feel every day, which isn't surprising considering how much time we all spend inside buildings. The average American, for example, spends 90 percent of their time indoors, yet so many of our buildings leave us without natural light, shelter us with low ceilings, and ignore our personal, social, and environmental needs.

It doesn't have to be like this. We can control this powerful force—we just have to start asking more from our buildings.

This architectural revolution is already upon us. The average person is more comfortable having an opinion about architecture today than ever before, mostly due to the dialogue enabled by social media. The world's 1.75 billion smartphones are fundamentally changing the way architecture is consumed, turning everyone into an architectural photographer. Photographs shared on social media liberate buildings from their geographic locations, enabling a new level of public engagement. We experience architecture today with an unprecedented immediacy, creating fodder for a global conversation about buildings and their impact.

This communications revolution is making us all comfortable critiquing the built environment around us, even if that criticism is just "OMG I luv this!" or "This place gives me the creeps." This feedback is removing architecture from the exclusive purview of experts and critics and putting power into the hands of the people who matter: everyday users. We have started "liking" and hating places out loud. Architects can hear us in real time, which has empowered (and sometimes even forced) them to pursue new ideas—to create solutions that respond to today's most pressing social and environmental issues.

In this new world, one in which people are asking more from their buildings, architects are no longer bound by any single style at any single time. People don't want their town library in Seattle to look the same as their grandmother's library in New Jersey. Even architectural historians don't know exactly what is going on right now because everything is changing so fast. In fact, they will never know what is going on again, because the future of architecture is a frenetic whirlwind of experimentation and a reevaluation of long-accepted habits.

This book considers the public to be a partner in architecture. The questions we can ask of buildings, and of architects, will create a new future—one that will look a lot different than the world we know today. Some of the questions this book poses may seem silly: What if a cow built your house? Can we swim in poop? Can we live on the moon? But two hundred years ago it was wild to ask, Will I live in the sky? Or, Will I need a sweater in the summer? Now that elevators and air conditioning enable us to live in the clouds and freeze in a heat wave, we must ask harder, more imaginative questions.

Architects have the know-how to design buildings that are greener, smarter, and friendlier—and now the public is a partner in this ambition. In one hundred examples, this book is a primer on how you and I and the entire world can ask for good architecture.

How we chose these buildings

The more than one hundred projects chosen for this book are a nonscientific and purely subjective collection of the most interesting and relevant work being done in the field of architecture. They represent every continent in the world and multiple building types. They are big and small, conceptual and concrete. They were initially culled from more than five thousand Architizer A+ Awards entries and supplemented by exhaustive research, conversations, and personal experience.

EXTREME LOCATIONS

Humankind's desire to explore and build in extreme locations raises a crucial question: How? How will scientists survive when they settle at the North Pole? How will naturalists take shelter when they observe reindeer in the Norwegian tundra? How will our children live when they land on Mars?

1 Can we live in the harshest place on Earth?

Forget outer space—scientists are still navigating uncharted territories here on Earth. This relocatable research facility sits on the Brunt Ice Shelf at the southernmost Antarctic station, operated by the British Antarctic Survey. Perched on giant ski-like foundations, hydraulic legs allow the station to "climb" out of the snow after heavy precipitation; when the ice shelf moves out to sea in warmer weather, modules can be lowered onto skis and towed to a new location. Setting a new bar for climate change research in the polar regions, its spaceship-like form draws much-deserved attention to this groundbreaking work.

Your survival depends on good design.

Halley VI Antarctic Research Station. Antarctica
HUGH BROUGHTON ARCHITECTS AND AECOM, CONSTRUCTED BY GALLIFORD TRY FOR THE BRITISH ANTARCTIC SURVEY

2 What does architecture look like above 10,000 feet?

Accessible only by gondola, this Austrian ski lodge sits 11,000 feet above sea level. It is designed to work with the natural landscape's sheer visual and physical power; the structure is perched on the mountain's summit to enable nature's unique "snow architecture" to accumulate and melt unimpeded. An abundance of glass windows allows for nearly 360-degree views, framed by a specially engineered floor and roof designed to withstand the elements and huge temperature swings of the setting.

Wildspitzbahn.
Tirol, Austria
BAUMSCHLAGER
HUTTER PARTNERS

Nature is the ultimate architect.

3 Can architecture be a path into the clouds?

These viewing platforms hover above the Trollstigen road, a mountainous tourist path that twists and turns up near-vertical slopes and perches on a dramatic pass between Norway's deep fjords. Humans may only visit—and build—there in the summer, when the weather is less harsh, but the platforms must withstand weather conditions year-round. Though the route delicately threads through the treacherous terrain, it relies on remarkable strength and careful engineering to stand the test of Norway's harsh elements.

Trollstigen National
Tourist Route.
Trollstigen, Norway
REIULF RAMSTAD
ARKITEKTER

The best architecture makes us forget how hard it works.

4 What do reindeer do all day?

A hiking trail leads to a spectacular site over-looking the Dovrefjell mountain range in central Norway, home to some of the last remaining wild reindeer herds in Europe. A sinewy pavilion invites visitors to warm themselves while observing the local reindeer population. The structure is an exercise in mate-rial contrast—a rigid outer shell of raw steel and glass houses a soft wooden core shaped like the nearby rocks, which have been eroded by winds and running water for centuries.

Architecture rewards the adventurous.

Tverrfjellhytta —
Norwegian Wild
Reindeer Pavilion.
Hjerkinn, Norway
SNØHETTA

5 Can modern architecture inspire pilgrimage?

The Ruta del Peregrino is a pilgrimage route that winds 72 miles through the Jalisco mountain range. Nearly two million people each year make the arduous walk to honor the Virgin of Talpa. This lookout point is one of nine pieces of architecture designed to provide landmarks and shelter for these travelers (and attract more casual visitors to the route as well). Balanced like a seesaw, it frames the view at one of the highest points on the trail and offers a moment of respite from the trail's harsh conditions.

Architecture can make the journey.

Ruta del Peregrino Crosses Lookout Point. Jalisco mountains, Mexico
ELEMENTAL

6 Can you dream beneath the Northern Lights?

This luxury hotel uses Iceland's otherworldly landscape to create a completely escapist experience for guests. The architects chose the location very carefully—local lore discourages disturbing cave-dwelling elves nearby. With the environment in mind, the architects made ample use of recycled materials; rubber tires were remade into bathroom basins and lava into lamps. A nearly infinite, yet sustainable, supply of hot water comes from a 190-degrees-Celsius hot spring heated by a nearby volcano. And when nighttime comes, the heavens above put on a show like none other.

Architecture reveals outer space on our own planet.

ION Luxury Adventure Hotel. Thingvellir National Park, Iceland
MINARC

7 Can a building stand on tiptoe?

At this desolate resort, the cabins are designed to encourage inhabitants to appreciate the isolation of the desert. Rather than planting each 20-square-meter EcoLoft hotel room on the ground like a traditional building, the architects designed them to hover over the land on thin steel supports. They are arranged like the boulders around the site, scattered in a picturesque composition.

Encuentro Guadalupe.
Baja California, Mexico
GRACIA STUDIO

Ecotourism needs ecoarchitecture.

8 Can an office float?

The Arctia Shipping Ltd. headquarters is a floating office building whose design references its neighbors: icebreaking barges docked on the Katajanokka shore, built to combat the region's extremely low temperatures. Its horizontal mass and customized black steel facades mimic the black hulls of the ships, while interior finishes of lacquered wood recall earlier shipbuilding traditions.

Arctia Shipping
Headquarters.
Helsinki, Finland
K2S ARCHITECTS

If buildings can float, whole cities could too.

9 Can a landscraper help us reach the stars?

In the Chilean Atacama Desert sits the Very Large Telescope, an instrument that's true to its name—it's one of the largest and most advanced pieces of optical equipment on Earth. At this flagship facility, operated by the European Southern Observatory, scientists working in severe climatic conditions (intense sun, extreme dryness, earthquakes) need lodging that will help them rest and recover between work shifts. This hotel is draped across the landscape, and has become a respite for those making extended visits to this beautiful, harsh environment.

Scientific progress requires healthy scientists.

European Southern Observatory (ESO) Hotel. Cerro Paranal, Chile
AUER WEBER

10 Can we live on the moon?

When we all eventually live on the moon, we'll need to be protected from gamma radiation. This four-person dwelling will do just that, providing shelter from huge temperature swings and meteorites. Inflatable domes give the structure its unique shape. Robots powered by solar energy will 3-D print moon dust (regolith) onto its surface, creating a protective shell that is ultralightweight because it requires no glue or other fasteners—its particles bond together naturally. Architects have created a 1.5-ton mock-up and have tested small modules inside a vacuum chamber. Look for the first structure soon at the moon's south pole.

Architectural ingenuity isn't earthbound.

3-D printed lunar habitations.
(Concept)
FOSTER + PARTNERS
WITH THE EUROPEAN
SPACE AGENCY

REINVENTION

It's bad enough to throw out a plastic bottle—imagine throwing out a whole building when you're done with it! New construction is wildly inefficient, which is why, for example, 90 percent of construction activity in the United States over the next ten years is expected to be on existing buildings. A grain silo becomes an art museum, and a water treatment plant becomes an icon. We can create a new future for our existing buildings by repurposing our past.

11 Can you shop in a cathedral?

As the number of brick-and-mortar bookstores in the world dwindles, the ones that remain have become sacred places to retreat. So what better place for a Dutch bookseller to reimagine itself than inside a thirteenth-century Dominican cathedral? The soaring nave allows ample space for a three-story-high bookshelf, which spans the length of the space and contrasts with the Gothic stone architecture around it.

Retail therapy can be a holy experience.

Selexyz Dominicanen.
Maastricht, Netherlands
EVELYNE MERKX,
MERKX + GIROD

12 Can rubble tell a new story?

Rubble from natural disasters is reborn, fittingly, as a history museum in China. Architects used the debris accumulated through earthquakes to build the facade of this building, commissioned by the city of Ningbo. Built in this way, the architects' vision becomes an icon of the past while advancing sustainable ideas of adapting existing materials to contemporary needs.

Bricks don't have an expiration date.

Ningbo Museum.
Ningbo, China
WANG SHU

13 Can ugly be pretty?

Newtown Creek is the largest of New York City's fourteen wastewater treatment plants. The city could have easily stuck with a utilitarian design, but instead it decided to put $4.5 billion into overhauling the outmoded and environmentally unsound wastewater treatment facility, following a design that is sensitive to the surrounding residential neighborhood. Working with a team that included lighting artists and an environmental sculptor, the architects created a complex that uses form, material, and color to create a striking visual composition.

Newtown Creek
Wastewater
Treatment Plant.
Brooklyn, New York,
United States
ENNEAD ARCHITECTS

Industrial architecture doesn't need to hide anymore.

14 Would you eat dinner in a sewer pipe?

Just try not to think about it—stacked precast concrete pipes traditionally used for wastewater become a dramatic, sculptural addition to an existing pub. Lined with wood, they create intimate dining nooks for those inside, and a sense of voyeurism for those who pass by.

Prahran Hotel.
Melbourne, Australia
TECHNÉ ARCHITECTS

Function follows form.

15 How much would you pay to sleep in a factory?

Repurposing factories into trendy hotels is happening around the globe—but this is a particularly striking instance of updated architecture bringing new life to a formerly industrial setting. On the East River in Brooklyn, the architects stripped and restored a brick, cast iron, and timber-frame building to create seventy-three guest rooms. A roof addition smartly uses contextual factory windows to create panoramic views of the Manhattan skyline while forming a visible icon on Brooklyn's own skyline.

Rest easy knowing you're cooler than everyone else.

Wythe Hotel.
Brooklyn, New York, United States
MORRIS ADJMI ARCHITECTS

16 How do you turn a grain silo into an art museum?

A historic grain silo composed of forty-two concrete tubes will become a museum on Cape Town's waterfront. The structure had no open space to begin with, so architects cut a cross section through eight of the central concrete silos (new concrete-cutting techniques will preserve their edges and add texture to the space). The effect is an oval atrium encircled by concrete shafts on every side. Artists will have the chance to create site-specific art in the silo's original underground tunnels.

Zeitz Museum of Contemporary Art Africa. Cape Town, South Africa HEATHERWICK STUDIO

A building can go from feeding mouths to feeding minds.

17 Can a bunker become a power plant?

In the landmark ruins of the World War Two-era Hamburg-Wilhelmsburg flak bunker, a drastic reimagining of the structure's purpose has taken place. It's now a green machine that converts heat to energy and almost wipes out its own carbon footprint. But its history hasn't been forgotten—located in the middle of a residential area, the bunker is also publically accessible as a memorial with a café.

Energy Bunker. Hamburg, Germany HHS PLANER + ARCHITEKTEN

Architecture reminds us that our memories are powerful.

18 Can superhighways make good houses?

We have all driven on highways without realizing their enormousness. This house awakens us to the scale of our transportation infrastructure. It's made using huge precast concrete beams that are traditionally fabricated for highway construction. A series of seemingly impossible cantilevers make us rethink our perceptions of gravity and scale. And check out that swimming pool!

Rethinking the obvious can create something entirely new.

Hemeroscopium House.
Madrid, Spain
ENSAMBLE STUDIO

19 Can a new skin save old bones?

When developers looked to transform a 1960s hotel into a high-end apartment building, their architects wanted to save as much of the building as possible while still upgrading its performance and overall image. They did this by creating a "second skin" for the building, which they installed onto the existing masonry facade. The new black aluminum panels host a vertical garden and drastically improve the thermal performance of the building (and look great doing it).

Good for the environment can be good for the eyes.

142 Park Street.
South Melbourne,
Australia
BRENCHLEY ARCHITECTS

20 Can historic cities have futuristic public spaces?

When Seville decided to replace the parking lot and bus station at its city center, officials were surprised to discover Roman ruins beneath the surface. What to do? Metropol Parasol was the winning scheme in an international competition that manages to protect the ruins, provide space for shopping and cafés, and create a grand new public square for the still-vibrant city. The six mushroomlike shading devices provide relief from the intense Andalusian sun, and visitors can climb to the top to take in a panoramic view of the walled city. Yet the craziest part of this swoopy landmark isn't its form: It is made mostly of wood and is the largest glued structure on Earth.

Cities are not time capsules.

Metropol Parasol.
Seville, Spain
J. MAYER H. ARCHITECTS

21 Can a subway station make you want to be underground?

This Budapest subway station extension was planned during the 1980s, but wasn't implemented until the new millennium. New construction techniques allowed the architects to excavate a giant box shape and use concrete beams to structure it. The haptic collection of columns, beams, and escalators is illuminated by the sun through a glass ceiling, making this subterranean space feel like a three-dimensional traffic intersection and transforming it into a valued public space.

Good architecture is worth the wait.

M4 Fővám tér and Szent Gellért tér stations. Budapest, Hungary
SPORAARCHITECTS

22 Can shipping containers be surprising?

Shipping containers—uniform in size, low in cost, available everywhere—offer an appealing building block for architects. Built to attract visitors to the Anyang waterfront's public art program, the APAP OpenSchool pushes the boundaries of what these modules can do. With one container skewed at a seemingly impossible 45-degree angle and another hovering 3 meters above the ground, the structure becomes a landmark within the city with the help of some bright yellow paint.

Architecture can invent extraordinary uses for ordinary materials.

APAP OpenSchool.
Anyang, Korea
LOT-EK

23 Can good architecture make 1+2=1?

The Museu de Arte do Rio and its adjacent school had an identity problem. The institutions are composed of three buildings: a 1910 palace, a midcentury bus station, and a former police hospital building. To create a single identity, the architects created a hovering concrete canopy to visually unite the disparate pieces. Thanks to barely-visible columns, the wave-like canopy seems to float over the museum campus, a bustling rooftop plaza, and the courtyard below.

With the right design, architecture can be more than the sum of its parts.

Museu de Arte do Rio.
Rio de Janeiro, Brazil
JACOBSEN ARQUITETURA

GET BETTER

Buildings impact our health and well-being. If you've ever felt depressed while sitting in a waiting room with low ceilings and harsh, flickering fluorescent lights, then you know the power of architecture over our psyches. The inverse is true too: buildings can have a hugely positive impact on the people who depend on them, from medical patients and doctors to students and the elderly.

24 Can a brick become a healing force?

In 2011, Butaro Hospital opened a 150-bed medical facility that serves nearly 350,000 people in this region of Rwanda. In spite of its impact, the hospital struggled to attract doctors to work there. The solution came in the form of these charming doctors' homes, which give foreign staff a permanent residence just five minutes from the hospital. In building the homes, architects took a truly holistic view of the community's needs and used the project as an opportunity to teach new skilled trades to the local community. On-site workshops taught

local teams to make compressed stabilized earth blocks—bricks that are earthquake-safe and sustainable. These teams also learned to make the hospital's custom furniture and light fixtures, as well as the earth-stabilizing landscaping techniques crucial to bringing agriculture to the region. With a total of nine hundred skilled laborers trained during the construction process, the effort brought better building practices, not to mention better medicine, to Rwanda for generations to come.

Buildings build futures.

Butaro Doctors' Housing.
Butaro, Rwanda
MASS DESIGN GROUP

25 What can a spa teach us about light?

A distinctive hotel built in 1967 has become a mainstay on the island of Majorca. Its latest renovation includes a new spa—one that relies on an innovative natural lighting design to completely transform the interior spaces. In the pool area, the building can finally take advantage of its sunniest facades via a roof and walls punctuated by arrays of strategically placed windows. In the spa rooms and workout area, huge glass windows let guests see the landscape, whereas smaller openings create a dark, serene environment in quiet areas like the sauna.

Hotel Castell dels Hams.
Majorca, Spain
A2ARQUITECTOS

Sunlight can be a transformative experience.

26 Would you die here?

This unique housing complex for the elderly reflects Portugal's cultural emphasis on quality of life. The human component is crucial in each piece of the design, which is based on a Mediterranean town—streets, plazas, and gardens are an extension of each residence. Translucent roofs light up as the evening falls, to ensure that elderly residents can move freely at night. This lighting scheme also becomes crucial in an emergency: triggering an alarm inside the house changes the roof light from white to red, signaling the need for help.

Light sends a message.

Alcabideche Social Complex.
Alcabideche, Portugal
GUEDES CRUZ ARCHITECTS

27 Can architecture help fight cancer?

A cancer-counseling center creates a microcommunity for visitors, caregivers, and counselors. With a jagged roofline that clearly distinguishes it from other hospital buildings nearby, the center is made up of seven small houses encircling two grassy courtyards. Here, patients and their families can learn, eat, exercise, and rest close to the main cancer ward, fostering close

collaboration between the hospital staff and
the Danish Cancer Society. Functioning like
a small community within the surrounding
neighborhood, the center highlights the
vital role that human contact can play in the
treatment process.

Architecture can give a healing touch.

Livsrum.
Næstved, Denmark
EFFEKT

28 Can architecture give us superpowers?

The secret of longevity? Intergenerational contact, constant physical activity, social interaction, fun, and happiness. All of these attributes are embedded in the Fun House—the centerpiece of the progressive aging community in Palm Springs. Key to this building is Madeline Gins's trailblazing theory of "Reverse Destiny": using structures to challenge physical and mental capacities, and viewing architecture as a key ingredient to a longer and healthier life.

Architecture can keep us young.

Reversible Destiny Healing Fun House. (Concept) Palm Springs, California, United States
ARAWAKA+GINS, REVERSIBLE DESTINY FOUNDATION

29 Can this school help autistic children learn?

This school is designed for students with autism spectrum disorder—students whose elevated senses can trigger traumatic responses to sudden transitions between physical spaces, as well as to large, undefined spaces. Nine residences and three classroom buildings are arranged to foster a therapeutic environment by allowing students to move gradually through the campus. Change in direction is signaled by soft turns rather than abrupt angles, slowly leading students to the doorway of each building.

Architecture can create beautiful choreography.

Center for Discovery.
Harris, New York,
United States
TURNER BROOKS
ARCHITECT

30 Can mud keep us safe?

Mae Tao Clinic is a humanitarian organization that provides free medical treatment, shelter, and food for more than three thousand children. Located a few miles from the Burmese border, the clinic needed to expand to make room for its increasing numbers. Members of this growing community built a new facility with local wood and adobe (mud bricks), which have been used as a weather- and fireproof building material in Thailand for centuries. Now, the new center is host to a healthcare education program that will create an even stronger social fabric in this border region.

Dirt can be the tie that binds.

New training center campus & temporary dormitories.
Mae Mo, Thailand
A.GOR.A ARCHITECTS

31 Would your kids visit you here?

Getting old shouldn't mean living in isolation. This home for the elderly is a hybrid of a hotel and a forward-thinking hospital. Each white cube apartment on the facade has a projecting balcony designed to shade windows below from harsh sun. This privacy is offset by the great public space the building is arranged around: The long building is a meandering path (you can literally walk on the roof) that surrounds a public courtyard where patients can gather and make new friends.

Buildings know there is strength in numbers.

House for elderly people.
Alcácer do Sal
Residences, Portugal
AIRES MATEUS

POP-UP

Scientists have laboratories. Architects have pop-ups.
These temporary structures are tiny experiments in form and space.

Can architecture pop-up?

Off-the-shelf acrylic tubes are assembled to create a rigid pavilion whose shape is inspired by a rough gemstone.

Bulgari Art Pavilion.
Manarat Al Saadiyat, Abu Dhabi, United Arab Emirates
NOT A NUMBER ARCHITECTS

Designed with emerging chefs and food truck culture in mind, a lightweight, corrugated plastic shell can expand to accommodate dinners for two or fifty.

PDU (Portable Dining Unit).
San Francisco, California, United States
EDG

A temporary floating wedding pavilion barely touches the ground, thanks to a balloon canopy filled with helium and draped in diaphanous fabric.

Floatastic.
New Haven, Connecticut, United States
QASTIC LABS

A temporary social hub on Governors Island at the Figment arts festival is made of 53,780 recycled bottles—the amount thrown away in New York City every hour.

Head in the Clouds.
Governors Island, New York, United States
STUDIO KLIMOSKI CHANG ARCHITECTS

Designers give a standard white party tent a makeover with a suspended landscape of white vinyl tubes.

Drift pavilion for Design Miami/2012,
Miami Beach, Florida, United States
SNARKITECTURE

SHAPE SHIFTERS

Can walls be invisible? Can a concert hall be a balloon? Can a skyscraper bend over and touch the ground? New technology for drawing, digital modeling, and construction means that architects are no longer bound by the shapes of the past, and can create unique spaces that look unlike anything we've seen before.

32 Can a building zig?

A border crossing is the first thing you encounter in a country, and the last thing you see as you leave. Georgia has built what must be the most interesting border crossing in the world, which is no surprise—since it was reborn as an independent democratic country in 1991, Georgia has been using architecture to rebrand its image to the world. Cantilevered platforms allow for viewing of the rugged landscape, and a cafeteria, conference room, and staff facilities are arranged to create a composition that promises wonderful discoveries in the country beyond.

The gateway to a country should entice and inspire visitors.

Border checkpoint.
Sarpi, Georgia
J. MAYER H. ARCHITECTS

33 Can architecture swirl?

An inflatable and mobile concert hall made of a stretchy plastic membrane brings both art and hope to earthquake-devastated Japan. The five-hundred-seat venue can inflate in under two hours and, when deflated, can move to a new location on the back of a truck.

The line between art and architecture can be a curvy one.

Ark Nova.
Matsushima, Japan
ARATA ISOZAKI,
ANISH KAPOOR

34 Can architecture swoop?

The Soviet Union was well known for its imposing and rigidly monumental architecture. When Azerbaijanis looked to create a new cultural center in their capital, they made an extreme departure from precedent. The building rises out of the landscape in a series of undulating curves to enclose over 57,000 square meters of space. The design represents the fluid relationship between the city and what happens inside the cultural center.

Heydar Aliyev Center.
Baku, Azerbaijan
ZAHA HADID ARCHITECTS

Architecture can create new landscapes.

35 Can architecture drip?

An international airport is an opportunity for a city to showcase its identity to visitors. That's why the architects of Terminal 2 in Mumbai's airport chose to reference the patterns of local jali window screens along its 17-acre roof. (*Jali* is the term for a perforated stone or latticed screen, usually with an ornamental pattern, often found in Indian architecture.) The coffered ceiling's pattern that drips into columns lets in light from above with skylights, creating a strong visual gateway to the nation's capital.

Architecture lets you know you've arrived.

Chhatrapati Shivaji
International Airport
Terminal 2.
Mumbai, India
SKIDMORE, OWINGS & MERRILL

36 Do buildings wear stockings?

In historic neighborhoods, new buildings should strike a balance between past and present architecture. For a new gallery in the northern part of Seoul, the architects created a white box that was ideal for the art inside, but too rigid-looking within its historic surroundings. A little wardrobe change did the trick: Wrapped in a flexible chain mail veil, the white box changes as light plays across its surface, better blending in with neighboring buildings.

Kukje Gallery.
Seoul, South Korea
SOLID OBJECTIVES-
IDENBURG LIU

A well-dressed building is never out of place.

37 Can architecture be from outer space?

The quickly growing city of Dalian asked architects to create a functioning conference and opera center, but also a visual landmark for the city—something that could become an icon for the local community and excite an international audience. The result is almost entirely self-referential, as if an alien ship landed on the banks of Dalian's port. The building doesn't look to context for its reference, it looks to the future. It's a hopeful symbol of what the city will become: a place activated by visitors, commerce, and culture.

Dalian International
Conference Center.
Dalian, China
COOP HIMMELB(L)AU

Architecture doesn't predict the future, it creates the future.

38 What if an office building turned inside out?

Office design can be hard. Columns and pipes often get in the way of the much-vaunted "open-plan" design that, in turn, can get in the way of cubicles and conference rooms. Not so at O-14, an office tower that relies on a white concrete bearing wall three feet away from the windows to carry the building's load. That means there are no columns in the space. The structural wall creates a chimney effect that pulls hot air away from the building (good in the Dubai heat), and with 1,326 holes in five different shapes arranged artfully along the building's length, it makes an elegant statement about this new type of skyscraper design.

A hole new way of looking at structure.

O-14.
Dubai, United Arab Emirates
REISER + UMEMOTO

39 Can glitz be more than glam?

When this 40-year-old villa was transformed into apartments, it was at risk of losing its singular visual identity. To retain its identity and upgrade it for better environmental performance, architects installed a reflective outer wall in front of the existing building. This mirrored wall protects the building from the harsh sun, while unifying the apartments behind a single, continuous material—one that reflects the beautiful landscape.

Mirror, mirror, be the wall.

Trevox Apartments.
Naucalpan, Mexico
CRAFT ARQUITECTOS

40 Is pretty a public amenity?

In case you were wondering, this shape is called a rotated rhomboid. Clad in sixteen thousand hexagonal tiles, this Rodin sculpture museum's muscular structure is wrapped in a shimmering mirrored skin. The pattern references Mexico City's traditional colonial ceramic-tiled building facades and, like those buildings, changes in appearance with weather and the viewer's vantage point, becoming a sculpture itself.

A museum can be as important as the art within.

Museo Soumaya.
Mexico City, Mexico
FR-EE / FERNANDO
ROMERO ENTERPRISE

41 Can architecture be an Olympic sport?

Ski jumping is a death-defying sport; athletes risk life and limb to launch themselves impossibly high into the air. The village of Holmenkollen, in Norway, has been home to the most legendary jumps of the last century, and a recent international competition aimed to raise its reputation even higher with a new sports

campus and jumping hill. Clad in stainless steel mesh and cantilevered 226 feet, the ski jump is the longest of its kind, making sure it is always the center of attention.

Architecture gives you wings.

Holmenkollen Ski Jump.
Oslo, Norway
JDS ARCHITECTS

42 Can architecture be pixelated?

A building that's a simple cube is complicated by a facade of square panels in ten colors—just like a pixelated image. The playful design breaks down the form of the office, but it also performs the serious task of concealing the proprietary research and development conducted by the technology company within.

Architecture can keep secrets.

Frog Queen.
Graz, Austria
SPLITTERWERK

43 Can stone flow like a river?

Inspired by the geomorphology of the Louisiana region's ancient riverbed, this museum's sculptural foyer uses 1,100 cast stone panels to form a pathway to the museum's interior galleries. The panels were designed and assembled using a custom automation process.

Technology is the new alchemy, turning rocks into water.

Louisiana State Museum and Sports Hall of Fame. Natchitoches, Louisiana, United States
TRAHAN ARCHITECTS

44 Have we been thinking about windows all wrong?

**The French call it a *brise soleil* ("sun breaker").
In Eastern architecture, it's a *muxarabi*.
Wooden screens have a universal appeal
for their dramatic appearance and serious
sun-shading ability in hot weather. At a residence in São Paulo, two huge wooden curtains
shelter the home of a young family, letting air
flow through and creating a private enclave
amid other houses. The best part is the mystery
of this seemingly "windowless" house.**

BT House.
São Paolo, Brazil
STUDIO GUILHERME
TORRES

Every element of architecture is ripe
for innovation.

45 Why can't walls be invisible?

**This is a museum for a glass collection, and
the architects decided that a building for
glass should be made of glass. The building is
composed of a solid floor and a solid ceiling
that appear to magically float on glass walls.**

Glass Pavilion at the
Toledo Museum of Art.
Toledo, Ohio, United States
SANAA

The boldest architecture is sometimes
hard to see.

46 Can a library be a mountain?

The illiteracy rate in the Netherlands town of Spijkenisse is a whopping 10 percent, so the city launched a type of architectural public relations campaign for books. Near the town square, community, educational, and commercial spaces were stacked into a pyramid, then wrapped with a 480-meter-long bookcase. Glass facades expose the library's collection, inviting everyone who passes to come inside.

Familiar buildings can still surprise us.

Stichting Openbare Bibliotheek.
Spijkenisse, Netherlands
MVRDV

47 Does a building need to be tall to change the skyline?

In Europe, residential buildings surround courtyards; in Manhattan, they reach for the sky. West 57th is the best of both worlds: its walls create a sheltered green space for occupants while maintaining the sweeping city vantage point offered by a skyscraper. Rising to a 450-foot peak, the building's shape lets sunlight deep into the block while keeping views of the Hudson River open for neighbors.

A condo tower doesn't need to be inward looking (and it doesn't need to be a tower).

West 57th.
New York, New York,
Unites States
ARCHITECT: BIG-BJARKE INGELS GROUP

48 Can glass be a fortress?

This concert hall is a collection of delicate crystals perched on the punishing Reykjavik waterfront. A collaboration with artist Olafur Eliasson, the building's south face is made of 823 "quasi-bricks"—stackable twelve-sided modules fabricated from steel and ten different types of glass that shimmer like fish scales.

But they aren't just a pretty façade—the glass bricks block noise from disturbing the performances inside. The strength of the glass combined with its structure makes this concert hall nearly impenetrable by the roiling nature around it.

Some materials have hidden powers.

Harpa Concert Hall and Conference Center. Reykjavik, Iceland
HENNING LARSEN ARCHITECTS WITH BATTERÍIÐ ARCHITECTS, RAMBØLL GROUP, AND ARTENGINEERING, AND OLAFUR ELIASSON

49 Can a light make a warehouse warm?

A warehouse is a warehouse is a warehouse, right? Well, not with a shape like this! The architects for KOP Warehouses replaced corrugated metal with corrugated transparent and translucent plastic sheets to let light in and out. The result is a simple twist on the traditional warehouse and proof that no building type is beyond innovation.

A smart architect can make a gem out of a lump of coal.

KOP Warehouses.
Puurs, Belgium
URA

50 Can a skyscraper bend over?

The new headquarters for China Central
Television (CCTV) combines the entire process
of TV-making—administration, production,
broadcasting—into a single loop of connected
activities. The building's form offers an alterna-
tive to the traditional skyscraper, encouraging
collaborative activities inside, and offering an
unprecedented amount of public access to
China's media production system.

New public engagement creates new forms.

China Central
Television headquarters.
Beijing, China
OMA

51 Can balconies make waves?

Architectural innovation can take huge amounts of resources and time to bring to fruition. Sometimes though, the answer is in the smallest details. Underneath its exuberant form, this 82-story hotel and apartment building is really just a traditional rectangular skyscraper. When it came time to design the balconies, though, the architect became a sculptor and created curvy and changing platforms that jut out from the building up to 12 feet. From a distance, this minor alteration creates a huge spectacle— a sensual cloud floating on the Chicago skyline.

Opportunity is in the details.

Aqua Tower.
Chicago, Illinois,
United States
STUDIO GANG ARCHITECTS

52 How much does interesting cost?

A site at a busy São Paulo intersection offered architects an opportunity to create a new city landmark—all while using traditional building materials and techniques to keep costs down. Balconies arranged seemingly at random are actually a simple extension of each floor plate, granting the design complexity and character without blowing the budget.

Innovative architecture can add value to a city without adding cost.

Top Towers.
São Paulo, Brazil
KÖNIGSBERGER
VANNUCCHI ARQUITETOS

DRIVE

There are over a billion cars on Earth.
They have to go somewhere.

GAS

Sometimes it's okay just to make
something beautiful.

Gas station.
Matúškovo, Slovakia
ATELIER SAD

No disguises necessary here.
The garage is a shapely icon that
is proud of its function.

Parking structure for the Tyrolean Festival Erl.
Erl, Austria
KLEBOTH LINDINGER DOLLNIG

A collage of photos taken in Venice
was translated into a four-layered design
to create a modern-day baroque
facade for this garage.

Facade of multistory car park.
Skopje, Macedonia
PPGA ARCHITECTS

A recycled stainless-steel wrapper encloses
the first LEED-certified gas station in the US.

Helios House.
Los Angeles, California, Unites States.
**OFFICE DA, JOHNSTON MARKLEE,
AND BIG**

It's a gas station, a restaurant, a public park, and a reflecting pool. Because why shouldn't gas stations offer true amenities to travelers?

Fuel station and McDonald's.
Batumi, Georgia
GIORGI KHMALADZE ARCHITECTS

NATURE BUILDING

Nature is an increasingly influential part of building design—we are being guided by trees, rather than overwhelming them. New architecture is finding innovative methods to incorporate natural landscapes into, onto, and around buildings.

53   Can you live in a rock?

With an entry and powder room fully carved from rock, The Pierre (French for stone) is a house that celebrates the rugged landscape of its site. Stone penetrates the structure—excavated rock was even crushed and mixed into concrete flooring—and construction involved dynamite, hydraulic chippers, wire saws, and hand tools. Rather than conceal this process, marks are left exposed to celebrate it.

The Pierre.
San Juan Islands,
Washington,
United States
OLSON KUNDIG
ARCHITECTS

Maybe cavemen were on to something.

54   Can you live on a rock?

A blackened-timber cabin built over the course of a few weekends gets a leg up from a boulder; inside, the incline turns into large steps that double as seating and sleeping areas, with storage underneath.

Tiny Timber
Forest Retreat.
Bohemia, Czech
Republic
UHLIK ARCHITEKTI

Bumps in the road can be a good thing.

55 Are treehouses just for kids?

A perfect 4-meter cube suspended midway up a tree trunk is a secluded living space large enough for two people. Its mirrored glass exterior lets it all but disappear into the wooded surroundings, but birds see and avoid colliding with it thanks to a transparent ultraviolet coating.

Architecture can wear camouflage.

Treehotel.
Harads, Sweden
THAM & VIDEGÅRD
ARKITEKTER

56 Can architecture hug a tree?

Architects have long considered the way different bodies move through spaces. Here, a woman who is confined to a wheelchair wants her home to revolve around the garden. This redesign of two 1830s brick cottages puts nature at the center of her family activities. Even from her wheelchair, she can enjoy views of mature trees from a home that is shaped to embrace them.

Design should work for all abilities.

Tree house.
London, United
Kingdom
6A ARCHITECTS

57 Can a tree house become a house-tree?

Vietnam's tropical forests have given way to dense cities—less than .25 percent of Ho Chi Minh City is covered in trees. To help residents reconnect with nature, architects broke a house into five concrete boxes and turned the roof of each one into a giant planter. If this idea is applied to other houses in the future, the green spaces could collect and filter enough stormwater to reduce flooding citywide.

House for Trees.
Ho Chi Minh City,
Vietnam
VO TRONG NGHIA
ARCHITECTS

Architecture can have a green thumb.

58 Can new buildings learn old tricks?

The plan for this visitor center began with a motif etched on stones uncovered at the former location of a South African trading civilization. Its free-form vaults were built with a 600-year-old construction technique that is both economically and environmentally responsible: Local laborers made the

200,000 pressed soil tiles as part of a poverty relief program. Though it's inspired by the past, the center's design is at home in the twenty-first century, with modern geometric forms that create a new topography in the ancient setting.

Modern construction can still learn from ancient techniques.

Mapungubwe Interpretation Centre. Mapungubwe National Park, Limpopo, South Africa
PETER RICH ARCHITECTS

59 Does balanced architecture need to touch the ground?

The shape of this house may be inspired by a traditional barn, but a dramatic 50-foot cantilever that lets it hover over the ground makes it a thoroughly modern feat of architecture; exactly half of the building is floating in the air. A rigid structure that uses a heavy concrete core where the barn touches the ground makes this possible. Underneath the giant cantilever is an epic swing.

Structural innovation, and a healthy budget, make the impossible possible.

The Balancing Barn.
Suffolk, United Kingdom
MVRDV

60 Can a lawn be more than ornament?

This building is a gateway between the busy city and the silence of the botanical gardens in Brooklyn. That's why it's half building, half landscape. And its roof is more than just a pretty feature—it's connected to a system that collects stormwater to facilitate natural filtration, and serves as an icon that attracts thousands of visitors to the garden.

Responsible architecture reconnects us with nature.

Brooklyn Botanic Garden
Visitor Center.
Brooklyn, New York,
United States
WEISS/MANFREDI

61 Can grass paint a city?

This five-story-high green wall incorporates 7,600 plants from 237 species to transform a historic corner in Paris into a piece of living architecture. Beginning with a plain concrete wall, the designer installed a metal, PVC, and nonbiodegradable-felt structure that prevents damage to the building while still allowing plants to grow without soil. A built-in watering system keeps the wall healthy, allowing it to mature and change the city landscape over the course of several years.

Le Oasis d'Aboukir green wall.
Paris, France
PATRICK BLANC

Plants help keep historic architecture alive.

62 Will the city of the future be a living organism?

In these fantastical renderings (produced for the History Channel's "City of the Future" Competition), plants become power producers that harness natural energy from the sun to power an entire city. As they grow, the plants take over the city and transform it into a hybrid place: part city, part forest. At the top, a canopy of biologically enhanced plants capture energy from the sun and water from the clouds. The canopy stays low in open, suburban areas and lifts off the ground in the dense remnants of urban downtowns.

MEtreePOLIS.
(Concept)
Atlanta, Georgia,
United States
HOLLWICH KUSHNER
(HWKN)

Urban planning meets the law of the jungle.

SHELTER
FROM THE STORM

Changing climates and weather mean danger—and opportunity—for our built environments. In the face of cataclysmic natural events, architecture is often the first line of defense. But architecture can also harness nature to empower inhabitants. With hundred-year storms now coming every ten years, and energy demands growing and changing exponentially, the world needs architecture that addresses nature in all its forms.

63 Can architecture retreat from a storm?

To avoid destruction during inevitable and intensifying storms, structures built within the coastal erosion zone of the Coromandel Peninsula must be removable. This house takes the requirement as a playful design challenge. The structure functions almost like a wooden tent—a two-story shutter winches open to form a sheltering awning, and closes to protect the house in inclement weather. Perched on two sleds, the home can move to the back of its site, or across the beach and onto a barge for a total relocation.

The Earth is changing, and so should our architecture.

Hut on Sleds.
Whangapoua, New Zealand
CROSSON CLARKE
CARNACHAN ARCHITECTS

64 Can we find salvation in paper tubes?

After an earthquake devastated the New Zealand town of Christchurch, citizens were left to grieve casualties as well as the loss of their central cathedral. One architect responded with a piece of "emergency architecture"—a rapidly built cathedral made of paper tubes, shipping containers, and a lightweight polycarbonate skin. The structure could not be more simple. The result is sublime.

Cardboard Cathedral. Christchurch, New Zealand
SHIGERU BAN

Rebuilding after disaster is a moment for ingenuity.

65 Can green infrastructure give us super powers?

This hydroelectric dam produces 10.5 million kilowatts of energy (enough to power three thousand homes), but that is not its most impressive feat! The amazing thing about this dam is the regard the architects showed for the project's surroundings. The architects considered noise, pedestrian paths, and even the water route that fish take. The sinewy shape makes it more than simply infrastructure—it is a working public sculpture that the city cherishes.

Protection can be more than security barriers.

Hydroelectric power station. Kempten, Germany
BECKER ARCHITEKTEN

66 Can playful be practical?

Our air quality is getting worse, especially in urban areas. Who can we look to for help? Meet Wendy. Wendy maximizes her surface area to expose as much titanium-nanoparticle-coated skin to the environment as possible. Every square foot of this surface sucks CO_2 out of the air—a total equivalent to taking 250 cars off of the road. The best part of Wendy is that she has a personality—she is big and blue and spiky, and she shoots out jets of water, and she has a name. The project was as much a social experiment as it was an ecological experiment.

Architecture can have personality *and* help the Earth.

Wendy: 2012 MoMA/PS1 Young Architects Program winner. Queens, New York, United States
HOLLWICH KUSHNER (HWKN)

67 Can we design for disaster?

In an area that was swampland two hundred years ago, the coastal play-grounds of Hunter's Point are prone to flooding in storms. The architects worked with the engineering team to anticipate this—the sunken oval playing field is designed to flood and act as a buffer for the rest of the park and the neighborhood beyond. It is a layered strategy that purpose-fully sacrifices playing fields in the event of a storm, rather than harder-to-replace infrastructure and houses.

Architecture helps us prioritize during a disaster.

Hunter's Point South Park.
Queens, New York, United States
THOMAS BALSLEY ASSOCIATES
AND WEISS/MANFREDI

68   Can architecture save us from the apocalypse?

Think of this as a safety deposit box for the world's seeds. Inside a mountain on a remote island halfway between Norway and the North Pole, this state-of-the-art storage facility provides what scientists believe is a failsafe way to protect food crops in the event of manmade or natural disaster. Built under thick rock and permafrost, the collection of millions of "backup" seed samples can remain frozen even in a power outage, securing the seed supply for centuries.

Svalbard Global
Seed Vault.
Longyearbyen, Norway
BARLINDHAUGKONSERNET

Give peas a chance.

69   Can architecture be a sponge?

New York has had some serious recovery work to do since Hurricane Sandy devastated its coastal neighborhoods in 2012. Six design teams have been chosen to develop innovative plans to protect the region from future storms. Plans range from huge berms that will protect the East River Park community from storm surges—while providing new recreational space—to green infrastructure that will store excess water and prevent flooding. Pictured here is the Big U, a series of green berms and landscapes to absorb storm surges.

The Big U:
Rebuild by Design
competition.
(Concept)
New York, New York,
United States
BIG TEAM, INTERBORO
TEAM, MIT CAU + ZUS
+ URBANISTEN, OMA,
PENNDESIGN/OLIN, AND
SCAPE / LANDSCAPE
ARCHITECTURE

Bad things can inspire us to do good.

70 How many ways can a roof serve a building?

With temperatures on the rise, roofs must be enlisted in the fight against climate change. In the spirit of technological advancement, this building will have what SHoP Architects calls an "Energy Blanket"—a roofscape designed to both collect and conserve energy using a range of innovative techniques, including solar panels, a water collection and recycling system, and huge

overhangs to shade the building's interiors. The mission of this 270,000-square-foot research facility is to support innovation and entrepreneurship in Botswana. It includes a data center, engineering floors, and an HIV research lab run by an international consortium.

Even incubators need shade.

Botswana Innovation Hub. Gaborone, Botswana
SHOP ARCHITECTS

SHRINK

By 2050, more than 80 percent of the world's people will live in cities. That means that every square foot counts.

How can we think smaller?

A polyester shell encloses an egglike multifunctional space. It includes a bathroom, kitchen, and niches for sleeping and storage. When the nose is opened, the whole structure becomes a porch.

Blob VB3
Mechelen, Belgium
DMVA ARCHITECTEN

This 914-square-foot transparent house is inspired by the concept of living in a tree, with twenty-one different floors at various heights to allow its owners never-ending variety.

House NA.
Tokyo, Japan
SOU FUJIMOTO ARCHITECTS

This 19-square-meter house has four rooms and was built for a quarter of the price of a similarly sized apartment in the same area.

Boxhome.
Oslo, Norway
RINTALA EGGERTSSON ARCHITECTS

A prefabricated, off-the-grid pod meets
need for safe housing in South Africa's
informal settlements, which house millions of
inhabitants in substandard conditions.

Mamelodi POD housing unit.
Pretoria, South Africa
ARCHITECTURE FOR A CHANGE

Part art installation, part artist's residence, this house measures 28 inches at its narrowest and four feet at its widest point.

Keret House.
Warsaw, Poland
JAKUB SZCZESNY

A tiny office wedged like a barnacle between two larger buildings allows traffic to flow beneath.

Parasite Office.
Moscow, Russia
ZA BOR ARCHITECTS

SOCIAL CATALYSTS

Cities are living organisms—without the right cultivation, they wither and die. Architecture has the power to stitch individuals into a community and energize forgotten corners of our urban fabric. Communities use architecture to plant a flag and rally together. Catalysts can be youth centers, religious buildings, libraries, and even beehives, but regardless of its use, architecture is a potent tool for encouraging the act of community.

71 Would you let your kids play in a wasteland?

Postindustrial wastelands don't always spark enthusiasm from local communities, but this project transformed a defunct warehouse and brownfield (land previously used for industry) into a public park and performance space with an amphitheater that rises like a wave from a wooden boardwalk. Now, this economically strained Virginia rail town has a new sense of pride that is rooted in nature, rather than industrial decay.

Landscape architecture can transform brown to green.

Smith Creek Park.
Clifton Forge, Virginia,
United States
DESIGN/BUILDLAB
AT VIRGINIA TECH

72 Can you swim in poop?

New York City is surrounded by water, but you wouldn't want to swim there—the city drains effluent directly into its rivers every time it rains. That's all going to change thanks to a crowdfunded initiative to build the world's first water-filtering floating pool. This giant Brita-esque pool will filter up to a half million gallons of river water each day, making the rivers cleaner over time and creating a much-needed public amenity that will reconnect us to the urban waterfront.

It's your city. You should be able to use it.

Plus POOL initiative.
(Concept)
New York, New York,
United States
FAMILY AND PLAYLAB

73 Can honeybees fight blight?

A colony of honeybees that had taken up residence in an abandoned building needed to be relocated. So a group of local architecture students designed them a new home in a 22-foot-tall honeycomb-shaped tower with perforated steel panels made to protect the hive from wind and weather. Inside, a cypress wood box with a glass bottom lets visitors see the bees at work from below. The new habitat is an educational opportunity for children and adults alike, who get to see the economic and environmental regeneration happening throughout this Buffalo neighborhood.

Hive City: Elevator B. Buffalo, New York, United States
UNIVERSITY AT BUFFALO SCHOOL OF ARCHITECTURE AND PLANNING

Underused urban areas can become hives of activity.

74 Can architecture feed a community?

Sitting atop a former twentieth-century factory, a 40,000-square-foot field is the largest rooftop soil farm in the United States. Part of a local for-profit initiative that now spans two rooftops in New York City, the gardens produce more than 50,000 pounds of organic produce each year for residents. It's local, organic, and takes advantage of a structure that was sitting unused for decades.

Brooklyn Grange. Queens, New York, United States
BROMLEY CALDARI ARCHITECTS

Join the roof-to-table movement.

75 Can paint unite a city?

This public artwork project began in 2010 as a collaboration between Dutch artists Jeroen Koolhaas and Dre Urhahn and a local team in Rio de Janeiro's Santa Marta favela—favelas are Brazilian slums or shantytowns—turning it into a more vibrant, appealing place. Since then, they have spread their movement across the

world, transforming a dilapidated area in North Philadelphia and working with communities in Curaçao and elsewhere to alter depressed public spaces in ways that will attract positive attention and economic impulses.

Positive change can come in a few cans of paint.

Favela Painting Project.
Rio de Janeiro, Brazil
HAAS&HAHN

76 Can color change your morning commute?

Just a few meters from one of Bratislava's historic squares, a dimly lit bus terminal sat neglected for years. To empower commuters, architects enlisted the local community to paint 1,000 square meters of pavement with green road paint. Two years later, they pushed the low-cost design intervention further with a crowdsourced lighting unit that was produced and installed with 4,000 meters of white packing tape. The resulting space is bright, cheery and a far cry from the drab station it once was.

An uplifting public space doesn't have to be expensive, but it does have to be smart.

Bus terminal under the bridge.
Bratislava, Slovakia
VALLO SADOVSKY ARCHITECTS

77 Can design help women thrive?

The nonprofit organization Women for Women International teaches war survivors marketable skills, empowering them to remake their communities. A designer collaborated with the organization to create a community center with an inviting public plaza—a meeting place designed to bridge the gap between urban buyers and rural farmers. The facility's sustainable systems are maintained by the women who live nearby, ensuring a strong local network that can support the community for future generations.

Architecture helps rebuild lives.

Women's Opportunity Center.
Kayonza, Rwanda
SHARON DAVIS DESIGN

78 Can opera empower a village?

In 2009, Burkinabé architect Francis Kéré teamed up with the late German film and theater director Christoph Schlingensief to bring an opera house to the rural area of Laongo. The two embarked on an incredible journey to heighten the cultural identity of the region, which was already the center of African film and theater. Still in progress, this "opera house for Africa" and educational center is already bringing together local residents and local materials to create beautiful music on a 30-acre campus that includes a five-hundred-student school and a health center.

A creative community is its own oasis.

Opera Village.
Laongo, Burkina Faso
KÉRÉ ARCHITECTURE

79 Can a garden shed unite a community?

A humble garden shed takes on a fantastic form to avoid casting shadows on nearby garden plots. Made of chemical-free materials, the building creates a shaded meeting space, while the charred cedar siding doubles as a chalkboard wall for messages and tips. The herringbone pattern of the wooden slats filter light into the interior while creating a trellis for seasonal vines.

Architecture is like gardening: You reap what you sow.

Woodlands Community Garden shed.
Vancouver, Canada
BRENDAN CALLANDER,
JASON PIELAK, AND
STELLA CHEUNG-BOYLAND

80 Can small housing be great housing?

Demographers predict that New York will add at least 1 million more residents by 2040—and many of these are expected to be one- or two-person middle-income households that won't qualify for city subsidies or financing. Sponsored by the mayor's office, the adAPT NYC competition sought new housing options for this growing population. This winning plan uses a solution of modular housing units that can be stacked to create fifty-five new microunits sized to 250 square feet. The concept can be adapted to many different locations, allowing city developers to meet the changing needs of citizens as quickly as cities grow.

Cities need homes for teachers and nurses, too.

My Micro NY: adAPT NYC competition winner. (Concept)
NARCHITECTS

81 Can architecture be crowdsourced and crowdfunded?

Mi Ciudad Ideal (My Ideal City) is an effort to crowdsource and document citizens' wishes for the future of their city and, eventually, to crowdfund them. Launched in Bogotá, Colombia, the program has already drawn participation from more than 130,000 residents. This new "bottom-up" approach to urban planning is well-suited to Latin American cities, where a huge boom in the number of middle-class citizens is requiring innovative solutions. The first example of this effort is BD Bacatá, a skyscraper created by Prodigy Network and sponsored by BD Promotores, that holds the world record in crowdfunding. It's a huge step in citizen participation and investment in a city's evolving needs.

130,000 heads are better than one.

Downtown Bogotá revitalization scenario from the My Ideal City initiative. (Concept) Bogotá, Colombia

ARCHITECT: WINKA DUBBELDAM, ARCHI-TECHTONICS

CREATOR AND DIRECTOR: RODRIGO NIÑO

PRODIGY NETWORK SPONSOR: VENERANDO LAMELAS

82 What happens when architecture keeps score?

In less than six months, architects of this Nike-funded football training facility created a place where twenty thousand footballers of all ages can play throughout the year. The first of its kind in Africa, the facility is designed to have an open feeling, but crime is a daily reality in this Johannesburg township. The building's transparency welcomes the community with invisible security at all times. The center has limited access points, and its wooden louver facade creates a tight perimeter outside, while huge expanses of glass face inward, toward the protected playing field at the center of the complex. Architects even commissioned the local artist Kronk to turn the security fence into a site-specific artwork, masking its true purpose.

Football Training Centre.
Soweto, South Africa
RURAL/URBAN/FANTASY PROJECT

Architecture should protect and serve.

83 Can a library be a lighthouse?

The new library of Alexandria is built on roughly the same site as the library founded by Alexander the Great 2,300 years ago, but the similarities end there. The building is composed of a giant slanted circle 160 meters in diameter. The glazed roof lets sunlight in at optimum levels to protect the books and wash the space with natural illumination. Like many modern libraries, the institution has expanded its mission beyond just books (though it can house up to 8 million of those too, and claims to have the world's largest reading room). With a planetarium, four museums, an information science school, and conservation facilities, the library has a new, more important role in the community than ever before.

A new roof can give an ancient library new life.

Bibliotheca Alexandrina.
Alexandria, Egypt
SNØHETTA

84 Can you get married in a parking garage?

There are over 105 million commercial parking spaces in the United States, and they are not always full. This Miami Beach parking garage creates a civic amenity out of its three hundred parking spaces. They can be repurposed when empty, thanks to super-high ceilings and amazing views. When the cars are gone, the building is used for yoga in the morning and is rented out for events at night.

Inefficient parking can create great public infrastructure.

1111 Lincoln Road.
Miami Beach, Florida,
United States
HERZOG & DE MEURON

85 Can a library be relevant in the digital age?

At the Seattle public library, the architects considered the way we consume media in a digital age and turned the library into a relevant public amenity by redefining it as an institution dedicated to more than just books. All forms of media—new and old— are represented here. They even redesigned the Dewey decimal system to make the place more intuitive and welcoming. The building's shape is a direct result of this rearrangement.

Libraries still have a lot to learn.

Seattle Central Library.
Seattle, Washington,
United States
OMA/LMN, REM
KOOLHAAS AND JOSHUA
PRINCE-RAMUS

86 Can you sunbathe underground?

Manhattan's High Line proved that an elevated rail line could have a second life as a vibrant public space. Now, a project called The Lowline aims to convert an unused trolley terminal into a subterranean hub for year-round events and activities. The plan uses a cutting-edge solar technology called a "remote skylight" to collect sunlight and direct it underground, allowing plants, and people, to thrive in a previously uninhabitable space.

The Lowline.
(Concept)
New York, New York,
United States
RAAD STUDIO

As urban spaces become scarce, we appreciate them more.

87 Can flipping a switch enliven a neighborhood?

This light and slender building at Paris Diderot University neighbors a hulking academic building next door. The new building faces a public square and acts as a bright gravitational counterpoint to the existing building. The open first floor beckons visitors in, and at night the entire building becomes a place-making icon for the university.

M3A2 Cultural and
Community Tower.
Paris, France
ANTONINI DARMON
ARCHITECTES

Opposites attract.

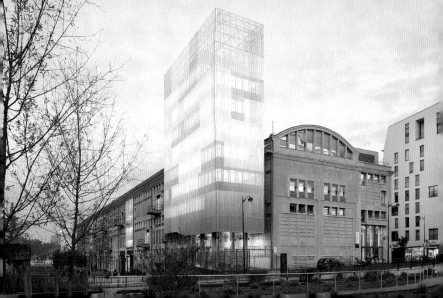

FAST FORWARD

We have been taught to expect the same thing from buildings over and over again: inert boxes made of concrete, steel, and glass. But in the near future, buildings will be wildly different than anything we experience today. This change begins with technology impacting our building materials, because the way we build impacts what we build. From 3-D printed houses to mushroom bricks, today's emerging technologies look beyond the hammer and nail to imagine a new way of constructing.

88 Can a building clean the air?

Welcome to the age of smog-eating architecture. Slated to make its debut at the 2015 Milan Expo, a 13,000-square-meter building will become an air purifier for the city, with a concrete facade that absorbs airborne pollutants and converts them into harmless salts that are then washed away by the rain.

Italian Pavilion.
Milan, Italy
NEMESI & PARTNERS

Architecture helps us breathe easy.

89 Can we print a house?

The 3D Print Canal House is an exhibition and experimentation site that remakes the typical Dutch canal house into a 3-D-printed home for the twenty-first century. The process of making turns digital files into physical building blocks using a KamerMaker, a large-scale version of a desktop printer. This makes it possible for the designers to create detailed components in a local style. The house is produced on-site, so there are no material transportation costs, and the potential for local manufacturing is high— meaning cities may no longer have to seek cheap building materials from far away as 3-D printing technology takes hold at the local level.

3D Print Canal House.
(Concept)
Amsterdam, Netherlands
DUS ARCHITECTS

Knowledge comes from making.

90 Can mushrooms replace stone?

These bricks are made of mushrooms. Mushrooms! The "bio-bricks" were grown inside of reflective trays made out of a mirrored film. These reflective containers were later used at the top of the tower to bounce daylight into the structure and the space around it. The tower's shape is designed to be efficient, too, cooling itself by pushing hot air out at the top. In contrast to the energy-gobbling skyscrapers on New York City's skyline, Hy-Fi offers a thought-provoking glimpse of the future. Hope you like mushrooms.

We can grow the future.

Hy-Fi: 2014 MoMA/
PS1 Young Architects
Program winner.
Queens, New York,
United States
THE LIVING

91 Can worms replace workers?

Silk doesn't seem like the sturdiest building material, but a group at MIT turned to 6,500 live silkworms to build a structure that connects nature with technology in a whole new way. They programmed a robotic arm to create a framework across a metal scaffold that gave the silkworms a roadmap to follow. When the worms were let loose on the structure, they responded to light, heat, and geometry, producing patterns that were a reflection of their environment. The resulting dome could inspire researchers to design and make man-made fiber structures never before imagined.

Architecture can imitate the beautiful efficiency of nature.

Silk Pavilion.
Cambridge, Massachusetts, United States
MIT MEDIA LAB MEDIATED MATTER GROUP

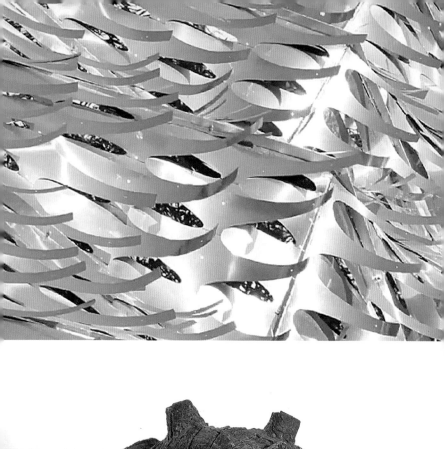

92 Can metal breathe?

The outside of a building, its skin, should be more similar to human skin—dynamic and responsive to the environment. That's the idea behind smart thermo-bimetal. Because it is made of two strips of different metals that respond differently to heat, this experimental building material requires no controls or energy to react to changes in temperature. When installed, its reactive property allows the system to ventilate on hot days, while shading it at the same time.

Humans breathe—so should our buildings.

Bloom.
(Concept)
DORIS KIM SUNG

93 What if houses were made of meat?

In the future you will be able to live inside a pig—sort of. No animals are harmed in the creation of Meat Habitat, a to-scale model of a house made with meat cells grown in a lab. The concept is a glimpse at replacing traditional building materials with pig cells that are 3-D-printed to create full-size architecture. And don't worry about preservatives. The skin is grown with sodium benzoate to kill yeasts, bacteria, and fungi—it will last longer than a Twinkie in its cellophane wrapper.

We could grow our houses by rethinking material structures.

In Vitro Meat Habitat.
(Concept)
MITCHELL JOACHIM OF
TERREFORM ONE

94 Can bacteria be your architect?

A 6,000-kilometer-long inhabitable wall in the Sahara Desert isn't built—it is grown, with the help of a bacteria that turns sand into sandstone. This is the concept behind Dune, a naturally generated sand structure that relies on a biological reaction: The sandstone is grown with the help of *Bacillus pasteurii*, a bacterial microorganism found in marshes and wetlands. Once introduced, the bacteria might be able to create a structurally sound and livable structure in less than a week, opening new possibilities for rapidly deployable refugee housing in the desert.

The desert is a living place.

Dune.
(Concept)
Sahara Desert, North Africa
MAGNUS LARSSON

95 Can architecture go wiki?

WikiHouse is a small experiment with a big idea: That regular people (read: not architects) can build a house anywhere with minimal tools and training. The open source construction system makes it possible for anyone to design, share, download, and "print" (with a CNC mill) quickly buildable houses from sheet materials like plywood that are low-cost but also suited to local needs. Continuously under development, solutions in the works include post-earthquake housing and a factory in one of Rio's favelas.

Design for the 100 percent.

WikiHouse.
(Concept)
ALASTAIR PARVIN

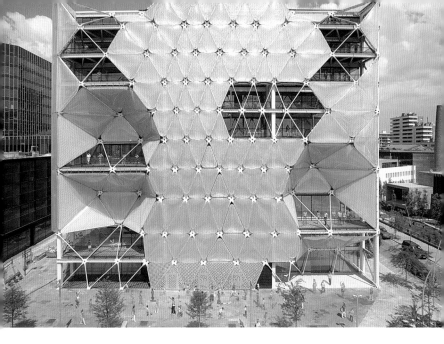

96 Can a building have reflexes?

The attention-grabbing Media-ITC building was designed as a collaborative space for the advancement of new technology. Its outer walls reflect this mission, with a translucent skin of temperature-regulating inflatable bubbles. Sensors automatically inflate the shading cushions to block light and reduce cooling costs on hot days, or deflate to let in more light on cloudy days.

Architecture made of air can help keep us cool.

Media-ITC.
Barcelona, Spain
ENRIC RUIZ-GELI/CLOUD 9

97 What if drones carried bricks, not missiles?

Flight Assembled Architecture is an installation built by flying robots. To build the 6-meter-high structure, a group of four-bladed helicopters carried fifteen hundred foam bricks and placed them based on digital design data that dynamically controls their behavior. This visionary approach to building is the result of a collaboration between architects Gramazio & Kohler and inventor Raffaello D'Andrea, who belong to a new generation of architects seeking to push the limits of digital design and fabrication.

Flight Assembled
Architecture.
(Concept)
Orléans, France
GRAMAZIO & KOHLER AND
RAFFAELLO D'ANDREA

No cranes. No ladders. No limits.

98 Can a skyscraper be built in a day?

Building a skyscraper used to take years. But a group in China is changing everything we know about construction, building a fifteen-story hotel in six days, then a thirty-story hotel in just over two weeks. The secret is prefabrication: Large sections of the building were assembled in a factory, eliminating waste and delays at the building site. According to the China Academy of Building Research, the tower is five times more earthquake-resistant than a similar one built with traditional methods.

T30 Hotel.
Hunan Province, China
BROAD GROUP

Even if buildings can happen in the blink of an eye, they should still stand the test of time.

99   Can skyscrapers be made of wood?

The idea of a wooden skyscraper raises eyebrows—and a lot of questions: Can it stand up in an earthquake? What if it catches fire? But this design competition winner proposes a thirty-four-story wooden skyscraper that would have the safety attributes of steel or concrete, with less construction waste and better acoustics than traditional high rises. The idea is more than speculation; Sweden's largest housing association plans to complete the tower by 2023.

New ideas can grow on trees.

HSB Stockholm competition winner. (Concept) Stockholm, Sweden
BERG | C.F. MØLLER AND DINELLJOHANSSON

100 What if a cow built your house?

To create this experimental structure, cleverly named **The Truffle**, a group of architects dug a hole, packed it with hay, and then poured concrete around it. **After the concrete dried, a calf named Paulina moved in, eating the hay for a year and hollowing out a small cave in the process**—all that was left in the end was the scratches and imprints of how the place was made. It is a fantastically hideous little building that became the most sublime place to watch a Spanish sunset. It's also a true melding of the most important tenets of future building: reliance on known techniques, forward-thinking environmentalism, whimsy, and brilliant simplicity. Moo.

The future of architecture will surprise you.

The Truffle.
Laxe, Spain
ENSAMBLE STUDIO

After journeying through these one hundred buildings, hopefully it's clear that there is no perfect, universal solution for the future of architecture. All across the globe, architects are eagerly working with clients and skilled builders to design unique buildings, tailored to changing environmental and social needs. They are pushing the envelope, barreling towards the unknowable future. And they need your help.

Don't be a bystander and let architecture simply *happen* to you. Find an architect. Study up on the latest ideas in architecture. Talk with the people designing the places where you spend your time. Talk with your neighbors, coworkers, friends, and family, and together, insist on good architecture.

Remember: Architecture doesn't just represent your community— it shapes your society. If you ask architecture to work for you, and to reflect the priorities of your community and the Earth, you will be amazed by the possibilities architecture can bring to every aspect of your life.

Happy building!

PHOTO CREDITS

AUTHOR THANKS

This book would not have been possible without the amazing work of Jennifer Krichels, who smiled all the way from Building 1 to Building 100. Special thanks to Matthias Hollwich, and to the teams at TED and at Architizer, especially Catherine Finsness, Siddharth Saxena and Luna Bernfest. To Chris Barley, the most patient speaking coach in the world—none of this would have been possible without your support. Thanks to the photographers for capturing all of this amazing work. Finally, thanks to the architects and their clients for designing and building such a magnificent group of buildings.

ABOUT THE AUTHOR

MARC KUSHNER is a practicing architect who splits his time between designing buildings at HWKN, the architecture firm he cofounded, and amassing the world's architecture on the website he runs, Architizer.com. Both have the same mission: to reconnect the public with architecture.

Kushner's core belief is that architecture touches everyone—and everyone is a fan of architecture—even if they don't know it yet. New forms of media empower people to shape the built environment, and that means better buildings that make better cities that make a better world.

Marc Kushner spoke at the TED Conference in 2014. His TED Talk, available for free at TED.com, was the inspiration for *The Future of Architecture in 100 Buildings.*

PHOTO: JAMES DUNCAN DAVIDSON / TED

RELATED TALKS ON TED.COM

Michael Green: *Why We Should Build Wooden Skyscrapers*
go.ted.com/Green

Building a skyscraper? Forget about steel and concrete, says architect Michael Green, and build it out of wood. Green explains that it's not only possible to build safe wooden structures up to thirty stories tall (and, he hopes, higher), it's also necessary.

Alastair Parvin: *Architecture for the People by the People*
go.ted.com/Parvin

What if regular citizens could design and build their own houses? The concept is at the heart of WikiHouse, an open source construction kit that means just about anyone can build a house, anywhere.

Thomas Heatherwick: *Building the Seed Cathedral*
go.ted.com/Heatherwick

A showcase of five recent projects featuring ingenious bio-inspired designs. Some are remakes of the ordinary—a bus, a bridge, a power station—and one is an extraordinary pavilion, the Seed Cathedral, a celebration of growth and light

Bjarke Ingels: *Building With Nature*
go.ted.com/Ingels

Danish architect Bjarke Ingels rockets through photo/video-mingled stories of his eco-flashy designs. His buildings not only look like nature—they act like nature: blocking the wind, collecting solar energy—and creating stunning views.

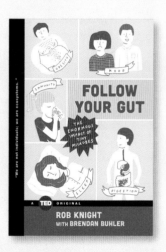

TED is a nonprofit devoted to spreading ideas, usually in the form of short, powerful talks (eighteen minutes or less) but also through books, animation, radio programs, and events. TED began in 1984 as a conference where Technology, Entertainment, and Design converged, and today covers almost every topic — from science to business to global issues — in more than one hundred languages.

TED is a global community, welcoming people from every discipline and culture who seek a deeper understanding of the world. We believe passionately in the power of ideas to change attitudes, lives, and, ultimately, our future. On TED.com, we're building a clearinghouse of free knowledge from the world's most inspired thinkers — and a community of curious souls to engage with ideas and each other. Our annual flagship conference convenes thought leaders from all fields to exchange ideas. Our TEDx program allows communities worldwide to host their own independent, local events, all year long. And our Open Translation Project ensures these ideas can move across borders.

In fact, everything we do — from the TED Radio Hour to the projects sparked by the TED Prize, from TEDx events to the TED-Ed lesson series — is driven by this goal: How can we best spread great ideas?

TED is owned by a nonprofit, nonpartisan foundation.

TEDBooks

The Art of Stillness
Adventures in Going Nowhere

PICO IYER

Photography by EYDÍS EINARSDÓTTIR

TED Books

Simon & Schuster

New York   London   Toronto   Sydney   New Delhi

TEDBooks

Simon & Schuster, Inc.
1230 Avenue of the Americas
New York, NY 10020

TED, the TED logo, and TED Books are
trademarks of TED Conferences, LLC.

First TED Books hardcover edition November 2014

TED BOOKS and colophon are registered
trademarks of TED Conferences, LLC

SIMON & SCHUSTER and colophon are registered
trademarks of Simon & Schuster, Inc.

For information about special discounts for bulk purchases,
please contact Simon & Schuster Special Sales at
1-866-506-1949 or business@simonandschuster.com

For information on licensing the TED Talk that
accompanies this book, or other content partnerships
with TED, please contact TEDBooks@TED.com.

Interior design by: MGMT.
Cover design by: David Shoemaker
Cover art by: Eydís Einarsdóttir
Series design by: Chip Kidd

Manufactured in the United States of America

10   9   8   7   6

Library of Congress Cataloging-in-Publication Data

ISBN 978-1-4767-8472-4
ISBN 978-1-4767-8473-1(ebook)

For Sonny Mehta, who has taught me, and so many others,
about art, stillness, and the relation between them.

TABLE OF CONTENTS

If I ever go looking for my heart's desire again, I won't look any further than my own backyard. Because if it isn't there, I never really lost it to begin with.

—Dorothy, *The Wizard of Oz*

Introduction
Going Nowhere

The sun was scattering diamonds across the ocean as I drove toward the deserts of the east. Leonard Cohen, my hero since boyhood, was singing so long to Marianne on my sound system when I turned onto the snarl of freeways that clog and clutter central Los Angeles. The sharp winter sun disappeared behind a wall of gray for more than an hour, and then at last I drew out again into the clear.

Turning off the freeway, I followed a riddle of side streets onto a narrower road, all but empty, that snaked up into the high, dark San Gabriel Mountains. Very soon all commotion fell away. Los Angeles simplified itself into a silhouette of peaks in the distance.

High up—signs prohibiting the throwing of snowballs now appeared along the road—I came to a cluster of rough cabins scattered across a hillside. A small man in his sixties, stooped and shaven-headed, stood waiting for me in a rough parking lot. As soon as I got out of my car, he offered a deep ceremonial bow—though we'd never met before—and insisted on carrying my things into the cabin where I was to stay for the next many days. His dark and threadbare monastic robes flew around him in the wind.

Once inside the shelter of the room, the monk started cutting up some freshly baked bread, to console me for my "long drive." He put on a kettle for tea. He told me he had a wife for me if I wanted one (I didn't; I had one on the way).

I'd come up here in order to write about my host's near-silent, anonymous life on the mountain, but for the moment I lost all sense of where I was. I could hardly believe that this rabbinical-seeming gentleman in wire-rimmed glasses and wool cap was in truth the singer and poet who'd been renowned for thirty years as an international heartthrob, a constant traveler, and an Armani-clad man of the world.

Leonard Cohen had come to this Old World redoubt to make a life—an art—out of stillness. And he was working on simplifying himself as fiercely as he might on the verses of one of his songs, which he spends more than ten years polishing to perfection. The week I was visiting, he was essentially spending seven days and nights in a bare meditation hall, sitting stock-still. His name in the monastery, Jikan, referred to the silence between two thoughts.

The rest of the time he largely spent doing odd jobs around the property, cleaning dishes in the kitchen and, most of all, tending to the Japanese abbot of the Mt. Baldy Zen Center, Joshu Sasaki, then eighty-eight years old. Cohen ended up sitting still with his elderly friend for more than forty years.

One evening—four in the morning, the end of December—Cohen took time out from his meditations to walk down to my cabin and try to explain what he was doing here.

Sitting still, he said with unexpected passion, was "the real deep entertainment" he had found in his sixty-one years on the planet. "Real profound and voluptuous and delicious entertainment. The real feast that is available within this activity."

Was he kidding? Cohen is famous for his mischief and ironies.

He wasn't, I realized as he went on. "What else would I be doing?" he asked. "Would I be starting a new marriage with a young woman and raising another family? Finding new drugs, buying more expensive wine? I don't know. This seems to me the most luxurious and sumptuous response to the emptiness of my own existence."

Typically lofty and pitiless words; living on such close terms with silence clearly hadn't diminished his gift for golden sentences. But the words carried weight when coming from one who seemed to have tasted all the pleasures that the world has to offer.

Being in this remote place of stillness had nothing to do with piety or purity, he assured me; it was simply the most practical way he'd found of working through the confusion and terror that had long been his bedfellows. Sitting still with his aged Japanese friend, sipping Courvoisier, and listening to the crickets deep into the night, was the closest he'd come to finding lasting happiness, the kind that doesn't change even when life throws up one of its regular challenges and disruptions.

"Nothing touches it," Cohen said, as the light came into the cabin, of sitting still. Then he remembered himself, perhaps, and gave me a crinkly, crooked smile. "Except if you're courtin'," he added. "If you're young, the hormonal thrust has its own excitement."

Going nowhere, as Cohen described it, was the grand adventure that makes sense of everywhere else.

● ● ●

Sitting still as a way of falling in love with the world and everything in it; I'd seldom thought of it like that. Going nowhere as a way of cutting through the noise and finding fresh time and energy to share with others; I'd sometimes moved toward the idea, but it had never come home to me so powerfully as in the example of this man who seemed to have everything, yet found his happiness, his freedom, in giving everything up.

Late one night, as my gracious host tried to instruct me in the proper way of sitting in the lotus position—rigorous but relaxed—I couldn't find the words to tell him that I'd never been tempted to meditate. As one who'd been crossing continents alone since the age of nine, I'd always found my delight in movement; I'd even become a travel writer so that my business and my pleasure could become one.

Yet, as Cohen talked about the art of sitting still (in other words, clearing the head and stilling the emotions)—and as I observed the sense of attention, kindness, and even delight that seemed to arise out of his life of going nowhere—I began to think about how liberating it might be for any of us to give it a try. One could start just by taking a few minutes out of every day to sit quietly and do nothing, letting what moves one rise to the surface. One could take a few days out of every season to go on retreat or enjoy a long walk in the wilderness, recalling what lies deeper than the moment or the self. One could even, as Cohen was doing, try to find a life in which stage sets and performances disappear and one is reminded, at a level deeper than all words, how making a living and making a life sometimes point in opposite directions.

The idea has been around as long as humans have been, of course; the poets of East Asia, the philosophers of ancient Greece and Rome, regularly made stillness the center of their lives. But has the need for being in one place ever been as vital as it is right now? After a thirty-year study of time diaries, two sociologists found that Americans were actually working fewer hours than we did in the 1960s, but we *feel* as if we're working more. We have the sense, too often, of running at top speed and never being able to catch up.

With machines coming to seem part of our nervous systems, while increasing their speed every season, we've lost our Sundays, our weekends, our nights off—our holy days, as some would have it; our bosses, junk mailers, our parents can find us wherever we are, at any time of day or night. More and more of us feel like emergency-room physicians, permanently on call, required to heal ourselves but unable to find the prescription for all the clutter on our desk.

• • •

As I came down from the mountain, I recalled how, not many years ago, it was access to information and movement that seemed our greatest luxury; nowadays it's often freedom from information, the chance to sit still, that feels like the ultimate prize. Stillness is not just an indulgence for those with enough resources—it's a necessity for anyone who wishes to gather less visible resources. Going nowhere, as Cohen had shown me, is not about austerity so much as about coming closer to one's senses.

I'm not a member of any church, and I don't subscribe to any creed; I've never been a member of any meditation or yoga group (or any group at all, in fact). This book is simply about how one person tries to take care of his loved ones, do his job, and hold on to some direction in a madly accelerating world. It's deliberately short, so you can read it in one sitting and quickly return to your busy (perhaps overbusy) life. I don't claim to have any answers, only questions that you can deepen or open further out. But I'd been reminded on the mountain that talking about stillness is really a way of talking about clarity and sanity and the joys that endure. Take this book, about these unexpected pleasures, as an invitation to the adventure of going nowhere.

1 Passage to Nowhere

When I was twenty-nine, I had the life I might have dreamed of as a boy: a twenty-fifth-floor office in Midtown Manhattan, four blocks from Times Square; an apartment on Park Avenue and Twentieth Street; the most interesting and convivial colleagues I could imagine; and an endlessly fascinating job writing about world affairs—the ending of apartheid in South Africa, the People Power Revolution in the Philippines, the turmoil around Indira Gandhi's assassination—for *Time* magazine. I had no dependents or responsibilities, and I could—and did—take long vacations everywhere from Bali to El Salvador.

For all the daily excitement, however, something inside me felt that I was racing around so much that I never had a chance to see where I was going, or to check whether I was truly happy. Indeed, hurrying around in search of contentment seemed a perfect way of ensuring I'd never be settled or content. Too often I reminded myself of someone going on and on about world peace in the most contentious and divisive of terms.

So I decided to leave my dream life and spend a year in a small, single room on the backstreets of the ancient Japanese capital of Kyoto. I couldn't have said exactly why I was doing this except that I felt I had enjoyed a wonderful diet of movement and stimulation in New York, and now it was time to balance that out with something simpler, and learn how to make those joys less external and ephemeral.

As soon as I left the security of my job and plunged into the unknown, my father began calling me up, unsurprisingly concerned, to berate me for being a "pseudoretiree." I couldn't blame him; all the institutions of higher skepticism to which he'd so generously sent me had insisted that the point of life was to get somewhere in the world, not to go nowhere. But the nowhere I was interested in had more corners and dimensions than I could possibly express to him (or myself), and somehow seemed larger and more unfathomable than the endlessly diverting life I'd known in the city; it opened onto a landscape as vast as those of the Morocco and Indonesia and Brazil I had come to know, combined.

I thought back to the day I'd wandered through an exhibition of Mark Rothko abstracts and felt myself drawn beneath the surface to a stillness that seemed bottomless and rich with every color; I recalled the time a friend had told me how John Cage had unearthed symphonies in the silences he'd set up in jam-packed auditoria. More than that, I'd long been moved by the way Thomas Merton, gregarious traveler, heavy drinker, and wounded lover, had stepped into a Trappist monastery in Kentucky and become Father Louis, taking his restlessness in a less visible direction.

Going nowhere, as Leonard Cohen would later emphasize for me, isn't about turning your back on the world; it's about stepping away now and then so that you can see the world more clearly and love it more deeply.

• • •

The idea behind Nowhere—choosing to sit still long enough to turn inward—is at heart a simple one. If your car is broken, you don't try to find ways to repaint its chassis; most of our problems—and therefore our solutions, our peace of mind—lie within. To hurry around trying to find happiness outside ourselves makes about as much sense as the comical figure in the Islamic parable who, having lost a key in his living room, goes out into the street to look for it because there's more light there. As Epictetus and Marcus Aurelius reminded us more than two millennia ago, it's not our experiences that form us but the ways in which we respond to them; a hurricane sweeps through town, reducing everything to rubble, and one man sees it as a liberation, a chance to start anew, while another, perhaps even his brother, is traumatized for life. "There is nothing either good or bad," as Shakespeare wrote in *Hamlet*, "but thinking makes it so."

So much of our lives takes place in our heads—in memory or imagination, in speculation or interpretation—that sometimes I feel that I can best change my life by changing the way I look at it. As America's wisest psychologist, William James, reminded us, "The greatest weapon against stress is our ability to choose one thought over another." It's the perspective we choose—not the places we visit—that ultimately tells us where we stand. Every time I take a trip, the experience acquires meaning and grows deeper only after I get back home and, sitting still, begin to convert the sights I've seen into lasting insights.

•   •   •

This isn't to suggest that travel is useless; I've often known stillness most fruitfully in a sunlit corner of Ethiopia or Havana. It's just a reminder that it's not the physical movement that carries us up so much as the spirit we bring to it. As Henry David Thoreau, one of the great explorers of his time, reminded himself in his journal, "It matters not where or how far you travel—the farther commonly the worse—but how much alive you are."

Two years after my year in Japan, I took some more concerted steps in the direction of Nowhere. Kyoto had given me a taste of stillness, but still I had to support myself by traveling, and in the previous few months I'd been lucky enough to journey all across Argentina, down to Tierra del Fuego, and then to China and Tibet and North Korea. I'd been twice in successive months to London and Paris, returning regularly to visit my mother in California. I had long, exciting voyages around Vietnam and Iceland coming up and felt more than spoiled for choice, able to refresh my engagement with the world every few weeks. But at some point all the horizontal trips in the world can't compensate for the need to go deep into somewhere challenging and unexpected. Movement makes richest sense when set within a frame of stillness.

So I got into my car and followed a road north along the California coast from my mother's house, and then drove up an even narrower path to a Benedictine retreat house a friend had told me about. When I got out of my worn and dust-streaked white Plymouth Horizon, it was to step into a thrumming, crystal silence. And when I walked into the little room where I was to spend three nights, I couldn't begin to remember any of the arguments I'd been thrashing out in my head on the way up, the phone calls that had seemed so urgent when I left home. Instead, I was nowhere but in this room, with long windows looking out upon the sea.

A fox alighted on the splintered fence outside, and I couldn't stop watching, transfixed. A deer began grazing just outside my window, and it felt like a small miracle stepping into my life. Bells tolled far above, and I thought I was listening to the "Hallelujah Chorus."

I'd have laughed at such sentiments even a day before. And as soon as I went to vigils in the chapel, the spell was broken; the silence was much more tonic than any words could be. But what I discovered, almost instantly, was that as soon as I was in one place, undistracted, the world lit up and I was as happy as when I forgot about myself. Heaven is the place where you think of nowhere else.

It was a little like being called back to somewhere I knew, though I'd never seen the place before. As the monks would have told me—though I never asked them—finding what feels like real life, that change-less and inarguable something behind all our shifting thoughts, is less a discovery than a recollection.

I was so moved that, before I left, I made a reserva-tion to come back, and then again, for two whole weeks. Very soon, stepping into stillness became my sustaining luxury. I couldn't stay in the hermitage forever—I wasn't good at settling down, and I'm not part of any spiritual order—but I did feel that spending time in silence gave everything else in my days fresh value and excitement. It felt as if I was slipping out of my life and ascending a small hill from which I could make out a wider land-scape.

It was also pure joy, often, in part because I was so fully in the room in which I sat, reading the words of every book as though I'd written them. The people I met in the retreat house—bankers and teachers and real estate salespeople—were all there for much the same rea-son I was, and so seemed to be my kin, as fellow travelers elsewhere did not. When I drove back into my day-to-day existence, I felt the liberation of not needing to take my thoughts, my ambitions—my self—so seriously.

This small taste of silence was so radical and so un-like most of what I normally felt that I decided to try to change my life a little more. The year after I discovered what a transformation it could be to sit still, I moved to Japan for good—to a doll's house apartment in which my wife and I have no car, no bicycle, no bedroom or TV I can understand. I still have to support my family and keep up with the world as a travel writer and journalist, but the freedom from distraction and complication means that every day, when I wake up, looks like a clear meadow with nothing ahead of me, stretching towards the mountains.

This isn't everyone's notion of delight; maybe you have to taste quite a few of the alternatives to see the point in stillness. But when friends ask me for suggestions about where to go on vacation, I'll sometimes ask if they want to try Nowhere, especially if they don't want to have to deal with visas and injections and long lines at the airport. One of the beauties of Nowhere is that you never know where you'll end up when you head in its direction, and though the horizon is unlimited, you may have very little sense of what you'll see along the way. The deeper blessing—as Leonard Cohen had so movingly shown me, sitting still—is that it can get you as wide-awake, exhilarated, and pumping-hearted as when you are in love.

2 The Charting of Stillness

Writers, of course, are obliged by our professions to spend much of our time going nowhere. Our creations come not when we're out in the world, gathering impressions, but when we're sitting still, turning those impressions into sentences. Our job, you could say, is to turn, through stillness, a life of movement into art. Sitting still is our workplace, sometimes our battlefield.

At the blond wood child's desk where I write in Japan, I have one constant companion, and he is alight with stories about glittery parties and the war, about ravishing beauties and society hostesses and bejeweled nights at the opera. But Marcel Proust could bring this thronged world home to me only by sitting still in a cork-lined room, nearly alone, for years on end, exploring the ways in which we remake the world in more permanent form in our heads.

That, in fact, was the idea behind his epic novel, the title of which is sometimes rendered as *Remembrance of Things Past*. We glimpse a stranger in the street, and the exchange lasts barely a moment. But then we go home and think on it and think on it and try to understand what the glance meant and inspect it from this angle and from that one, spinning futures and fantasies around it. The experience that lasted an instant plays out for a lifetime inside us. It becomes, in fact, the story of our lives.

My other loyal companion in Japan, as he has been since I was a teenager traveling from Dharamsala to Bogotá and Barbados, is, as it happens, the roaming troubadour whose debut album had featured four songs with the word "travel" at their center. The first song Leonard Cohen ever delivered in public was about a man taking out an old train schedule, a highway "curling up like smoke above his shoulder." One of the most heartfelt numbers on that maiden record found him saying good-bye to a woman because he had to "wander in my time."

Leonard Cohen had become the poet laureate of those on the road, refusing to stick to any form of settling down, a "gypsy boy" who wouldn't sit still within any of the expectations we brought to him. But, like many a wanderer, he seemed always to know that it's only when you stop moving that you can be moved in some far deeper way ("Now I know why many men have stopped and wept," he writes in an early poem, "Halfway between the loves they leave and seek, / And wondered if travel leads them anywhere").

Whenever he took his pulse most directly, he tended to acknowledge that his greatest journeys were inner ones. "I needed so much to have nothing to touch," he confesses in one typically unflinching song about going to the Zen Center. "I've always been greedy that way."

• • •

Almost a decade after my first visit to Leonard Cohen's perch in the bare hall near the top of the mountain, I ran into another unlikely maverick, this time in Zürich. I was in the Hallenstadion, a thirteen-thousand-seat auditorium recently visited by Britney Spears, where the Fourteenth Dalai Lama, on whose global movements I was writing, was delivering a complex discourse on the Bodhisattva's way of life, explaining why some humans who attain Nirvana (the word means "blown out" in Sanskrit) choose to come back to the world to help the rest of us.

Many of the native English speakers there—mostly Buddhist, as I am not—were trying, if they could, to follow the intricate philosophical teachings in French, in part because the Dalai Lama's words came through his French translator with such lucid transparency. The translator's name was Matthieu Ricard, and he'd received his PhD in molecular biology from the Institut Pasteur, studying under the Nobel Prize winner François Jacob. Indeed, Matthieu's father, Jean-François Revel, was celebrated as one of France's leading intellectuals, the longtime editor of *L'Express*; his mother, Yahne le Toumelin, was well known for her abstract art. Around the family dinner table, while Matthieu was growing up, sat Buñuel and Stravinsky and Cartier-Bresson.

But when he was twenty-one, Ricard took a trip to

Nepal, and the joy and sense of discernment he'd encountered in and through some Tibetan lamas there
had so profoundly moved him that, five years on, he
abandoned his promising career in science and went
to live in the shadow of the Himalayas. He learned Tibetan, took on monastic robes, and served—for more
than a dozen years—as attendant and student of the
Tibetan teacher Dilgo Khyentse Rinpoche. At one point
in the mid-1990s, Matthieu's father flew to Nepal to
spend ten days in dialogue with his scientist son to find
out why his offspring would write (much as Leonard
Cohen might) that "Simplifying one's life to extract its
quintessence is the most rewarding of all the pursuits I
have undertaken."

The book that arose out of their discussions, *The
Monk and the Philosopher*, sold almost half a million
copies in France, in part because Ricard was able to
argue for the Buddhist "science of mind" he had taken
on with all the Cartesian clarity and eloquence he'd no
doubt inherited from his father. No one I'd met could
better explain, for example, how getting caught up in
the world and expecting to find happiness there made
about as much sense as reaching into a fire and hoping
not to get burned.

Just before I met him, Ricard had been the first par-
ticipant in an experiment conducted by researchers at
the University of Wisconsin. Scientists had attached
256 electrodes to the skulls of hundreds of volun-
teers and put them through a three-and-a-half-hour

continuous functional MRI scan to test for positive emotions (and, in later experiments, compassion, the ability to control emotional responses, the capacity to process information). The subjects were similar in every respect except that some had given themselves over to a regular practice of stillness and the others had not. Ricard's score for positive emotions was so far beyond the average of nonmonastic subjects that the researchers, after testing many others who had meditated for ten thousand hours or more and many who had not, felt obliged to conclude that those who had sat still for years had achieved a level of happiness that was, quite literally, off the charts, unseen before in the neurological literature.

By the time we met in Zürich, the fifty-nine-year-old Frenchman was routinely described as "the happiest man in the world." He was also in constant demand, explaining how happiness can be developed just as any muscle can be at the World Economic Forum in Davos, participating in conferences between scientists of matter and of mind in India, translating for the Dalai Lama across the globe, bringing the priorities he'd sharpened in stillness to the construction of clinics and schools and bridges across Tibet. Soon after we first got to know each other, I asked him a typical traveler's question: How did he deal with jet lag? He looked at me, surprised. "For me a flight is just a brief retreat in the sky," Matthieu said, as if amazed that the idea didn't strike everyone. "There's nothing I can do, so it's really quite liberating. There's nowhere else I can be. So I just sit and watch the clouds and the blue sky. Everything is still and everything is moving. It's beautiful." Clouds and blue sky, of course, are how Buddhists explain the nature of our mind: there may be clouds passing across it, but that doesn't mean a blue sky isn't always there behind the obscurations. All you need is the patience to sit still until the blue shows up again.

His explanation made a different kind of sense a few years later, when Ricard published a book of photographs that looked to me like the ultimate travel book. He'd been on retreat in a cabin on top of a mountain in Nepal for the better part of a year, and once or twice a week, he'd stepped outside and taken a picture of what lay beyond his front door. The same view, more or less, but as it changed with clouds or rain, in winter or in spring, and as the moods of the man behind the lens changed.

When I paged through the book, I realized Matthieu had inherited his mother's eye for the art of stillness as well as his father's analytical mind; these Portraits of Nowhere, as they could have been called, were magical. I saw Indonesia and Peru, sunlit valleys and storm-blackened skies in his work; it felt as if most of the world had made a house call to his cabin. The book, which he called *Motionless Journey*, might almost have been an investigation into how everything changes and doesn't change at all—how the same place looks different even as you're not really going anywhere.

But what made it most haunting was that, at heart, it was a description of an inner landscape. This is what your mind—your life—looks like when you're going nowhere. Always full of new colors, sights, and beauties; always, more or less, unaltered.

3 Alone in the Dark

None of us, of course, would want to be in a Nowhere we hadn't chosen, as prisoners or invalids are. Whenever I travel to North Korea or Yemen—to any of the world's closed or impoverished places—I see how almost anyone born to them would long to be anywhere else, and to visit other countries with the freedom that some of the rest of us enjoy. From San Quentin to New Delhi, the incarcerated are taught meditation, but only so they can see that within their confinement there may be spots of liberation. Otherwise, those in solitary may find themselves bombarded by the terrors and unearthly visitations that Emily Dickinson knew in her "still—Volcano—Life."

I once went into the woods of Alberta and sat in a cabin day after day with letters from Dickinson, the poet famous for seldom leaving her home. Her passion shook me till I had to look away, the feeling was so intense and caged; her words were explosives in a jewel box. I imagined standing with the woman in white at her window, watching her brother with his young wife, Susan—to whom Dickinson addressed some of her most passionate letters ("Oh my darling one"; "my heart is full of you, none other than you is in my thoughts")—in the house they shared one hundred yards away, across the garden.

I felt her slipping through her parlor while her brother conducted an adulterous affair in the next room, betraying the Sue they both adored. I saw her crafting, in a fury, her enflamed letters to her "Master," the atmosphere charged around her in her solitude, or writing, "I see thee better—in the Dark."

She could feel Death calling for her in her bed, she wrote, as she plumbed the shadows within the stillness; again and again she imagined herself posthumous, mourners "treading—treading" in her brain. She knew that you do not have to be a chamber to be haunted, that "Ourself behind ourself concealed— / Should startle most." Her unsettling words brought to mind poor Herman Melville, conjuring up at the same time his own version of a motionless ghost, Bartleby, a well-spoken corpse conducting a makeshift Occupy Wall Street resistance by sitting in a lawyer's office in lower Manhattan, "preferring" not to go anywhere.

Nowhere can be scary, even if it's a destination you've chosen; there's nowhere to hide there. Being locked inside your head can drive you mad or leave you with a devil who tells you to stay at home and stay at home till you are so trapped inside your thoughts that you can't step out or summon the power of intention.

A life of stillness can sometimes lead not to art but to doubt or dereliction; anyone who longs to see the light is signing on for many long nights alone in the dark. Visiting a monastery, I also realized how easy it might be to go there as an escape, or in the throes of an infatuation certain not to last. As in any love affair, the early days of a romance with stillness give little sign of the hard work to come.

Sometimes, when I returned to my monastery in midwinter, the weather was foul as I pulled up. The rain pattered down on the tin roof of my trailer throughout the night. The view through the picture windows was of nothing but mist. I didn't see or hear a living soul for days on end, and my time felt like a trial, a penitential exercise in loneliness. The downpour was so unending that I couldn't go out, and so I sat in the fog, stuck and miserable, reminded how the external environment can too easily be a reflection of—sometimes a catalyst for—an inner one.

"The way of contemplation is not even a way," as Thomas Merton, the eloquent monk, put it, "and if one follows it, what he finds is nothing." One of the laws of sitting still, in fact, is that "if you enter it with the set purpose of seeking contemplation, or, worse still, happiness, you will find neither. For neither can be found unless it is first in some sense renounced." This was all a bit paradoxical—as hard to disentangle as a Zen koan—but I could catch the fundamental point: a man sitting still is alone, often, with the memory of all he doesn't have. And what he does have can look very much like nothing.

• • •

One morning in early summer, when I was visiting Louisville, Kentucky, a new friend offered to drive me out to see the monastery where Thomas Merton had lived for more than a quarter of a century. Very soon the city was far behind us, and we were passing empty green fields and the occasional house with a cross (or words from the Bible) outside it. When we got to the place Merton had made so famous—a place that looked grave and forbidding, like a dark Victorian asylum for the mentally troubled—a tall, quiet monk who had studied under Merton offered to show us the hermitage where Father Louis (as Merton was still known there) had spent much of his last two years, having found even the monastery too full of distraction and commotion.

We walked past graves and across a field. "For the last three years," said the monk, fresh and quickly striding though in his early seventies, "I've been in love." He paused. "With a woman named Emily Dickinson."

We let this pass, and followed the man in robes to a rather rickety little cabin "in the shadow of a big cedar cross," as Merton had described it, a barn adjoining it and a tiny porch with a single chair in front of it.

Inside, the place was modestly furnished, though spacious by monastic standards. Our tour guide sat down and proceeded to recite some lines from Rainer Maria Rilke. "Always there is World," the German poet put it, "and never Nowhere without the No: that pure unseparated element which one breathes without desire and endlessly *knows*."

Then, from Dickinson:

The Brain—is wider than the Sky—
For—put them side by side—
The one the other will contain
With ease—and You—beside—

Then he got up and picked out a book at random from the shelves. "I like to read something from Father Louis's journals whenever I show people this place," the monk said. "To bring his spirit into our company. So we can feel he's here."

He opened to a random page and began to read.

"We ate herring and ham (not very much eating!) and drank our wine and read poems and talked of ourselves and mostly made love and love and love for five hours. Though we had over and over reassured ourselves and agreed that our love would have to continue always chaste and this sacrifice was essential, yet in the end we were getting rather sexy. Yet really, instead of being all wrong, it seemed eminently right. We now love with our whole bodies anyway, and I have the complete feel of her being (except her sex) as completely me."

It was a passage from Volume 5 of the printed journals, perhaps the most startling section of the sometimes angry monk's meditations. At fifty-one, Merton had gone into St. Joseph's Hospital in Louisville for back surgery. He'd scorned the trip in advance—"I do not expect much help from doctors and their damned pills"—and, the morning before he left, he wrote, as if to reassure himself, "I am just beginning to get grounded in solitude." His one regret, should he die, he wrote, would be the "loss of the years of solitude that might be possible." But while in the hospital, he very quickly—after almost a quarter-century out of the world—fell tumultuously in love with the "very friendly and devoted" twenty-year-old student nurse who was helping to take care of him.

The hundreds of pages in his diary in which he thrashed out his feelings for her are agonizing to read; it's as if this wise man who knew so much about stillness and truth became an adolescent boy again, twisting and turning on his bed as he tried to sort out a kind of love he hadn't known since taking a vow of chastity. He started bombarding the young woman with letters and naked entreaties, made unlicensed phone calls to her from the cellarer's office while his brother monks were at dinner. When another monk overheard him, he confessed to his long-suffering abbot ("about the phone calls *only!*"), but still kept talking of forfeiting his vocation to run away with "M." and live with her on an island.

"I am flooded with peace (whereas last Sunday the mere idea that this might happen tore me with anguish and panic)," Merton wrote. "I have surrendered again to a kind of inimical womanly wisdom in M. which instinctively seeks out the wound in me that most needs her sweetness and lavishes all her love upon me there. Instead of feeling impure, I feel purified (which is in fact what I myself wrote the other day in the "Seven Words" for Ned O'Gorman). I feel that somehow my sexuality has been made real and decent again after years of rather frantic suppression (for though I thought I had it all truly controlled, this was an illusion)."

Our monk, to his credit, kept reading the passage to its end, never faltering or deciding that some other passage might be more profitable. Just one year before meeting "M.," ecstatic in his new hermitage, Merton had written, "I had decided to marry the silence of the forest. The sweet dark warmth of the whole world will have to be my wife." That, too, seemed to have changed, like the skies in Matthieu Ricard's photos. You don't get over the shadows inside you simply by walking away from them.

4 Stillness Where It's Needed Most

The idea of going nowhere is, as mentioned, as universal as the law of gravity; that's why wise souls from every tradition have spoken of it. "All the unhappiness of men," the seventeenth-century French mathematician and philosopher Blaise Pascal famously noted, "arises from one simple fact: that they cannot sit quietly in their chamber." After Admiral Richard E. Byrd spent nearly five months alone in a shack in the Antarctic, in temperatures that sank to 70 degrees below zero, he emerged convinced that "Half the confusion in the world comes from not knowing how little we need." Or, as they sometimes say around Kyoto, "Don't just do something. Sit there."

Yet the days of Pascal and even Admiral Byrd seem positively tranquil by today's standards. The amount of data humanity will collect while you're reading this book is five times greater than the amount that exists in the entire Library of Congress. Anyone reading this book will take in as much information today as Shakespeare took in over a lifetime. Researchers in the new field of interruption science have found that it takes an average of twenty-five minutes to recover from a phone call. Yet such interruptions come every eleven minutes—which means we're never caught up with our lives.

And the more facts come streaming in on us, the less time we have to process any one of them. The one thing technology doesn't provide us with is a sense of how to make the best use of technology. Put another way, the ability to gather information, which used to be so crucial, is now far less important than the ability to sift through it.

It's easy to feel as if we're standing two inches away from a huge canvas that's noisy and crowded and changing with every microsecond. It's only by stepping farther back and standing still that we can begin to see what that canvas (which is our life) really means, and to take in the larger picture.

●　●　●

As I travel the world, one of the greatest surprises I have encountered has been that the people who seem wisest about the necessity of placing limits on the newest technologies are, often, precisely the ones who helped develop those technologies, which have bulldozed over so many of the limits of old. The very people, in short, who have worked to speed up the world are the same ones most sensitive to the virtue of slowing down.

One day I visited Google's headquaters to give a talk on the Dalai Lama book I'd completed and, like most visitors, was much impressed by the trampolines, the indoor tree houses, and the workers at the time enjoying a fifth of their working hours free, letting their minds wander off leash to where inspiration might be hiding.

But what impressed me even more were the two people who greeted me as I waited for my digital ID: the Chief Evangelist for Google+, as his business card would have it, a bright-eyed, visibly spirited young soul from India who was setting up a "Yogler" program whereby the many Googlers who practice yoga could actually be trained to teach it; and the seasoned software engineer beside him who ran a celebrated and popular seven-week program called "Search Inside Yourself," whose curriculum had shown more than a thousand Googlers the quantifiable, scientific evidence that meditation could lead not just to clearer thinking and better health but to emotional intelligence.

A self-selecting pair, no doubt; these were the kind of guys who wanted to hear about the Dalai Lama. Every company has its own chief evangelists, eager to share their illuminations. But I was struck by how often Gopi, the founder of the Yogler program, spoke of how easy it was, day or night, to go into a conference room and close his eyes. It sounded a bit like Dickinson again:

> The Outer—from the Inner
> Derives its Magnitude—
> 'Tis Duke, or Dwarf, according
> As is the Central Mood.

Many in Silicon Valley observe an "Internet Sabbath" every week, during which they turn off most of their devices from, say, Friday night to Monday morning, if only to regather the sense of proportion and direction they'll need for when they go back online. I was reminded of this by Kevin Kelly, one of the most passionate spokesmen for new technologies (and the founding executive editor of *Wired* magazine), who had written his latest book about how technology can "expand our individual potential" while living without a smartphone, a laptop, or a TV in his home. Kevin still takes off on months-long trips through Asian villages without a computer, so as to be rooted in the nonvirtual world. "I continue to keep the cornucopia of technology at arm's length," he writes, "so that I can more easily remember who I am."

There is now a meditation room in every building on the General Mills campus in Minneapolis, and Congressman Tim Ryan leads his colleagues in the House of Representatives in sessions of sitting still, reminding them that, if nothing else, it's been found by scientists that meditation can lower blood pressure, help boost our immune system, and even change the architecture of our brains. This has no more to do with religion or any other kind of doctrine than a trip to the (mental) health club might.

Indeed, fully a third of American companies now have "stress-reduction programs," and the number is increasing by the day—in part because workers find unclogging their minds' arteries to be so exhilarating. More than 30 percent of those enrolled in such a program at Aetna, the giant heath-care company, saw their levels of stress dropping by a third after only an hour of yoga each week. The computer chip maker Intel experimented with a "Quiet Period" of four hours every Tuesday, during which three hundred engineers and managers were asked to turn off their e-mail and phones and put up "Do Not Disturb" signs on their office doors in order to make space for "thinking time." The response proved so enthusiastic that the company inaugurated an eight-week program to encourage clearer thinking. At General Mills, 80 percent of senior executives reported a positive change in their ability to make decisions, and 89 percent said that they had become better listeners, after a similar seven-week program. Such developments are saving American corporations three hundred billion dollars a year; more important, they're a form of preemptive medicine at a time when the World Health Organization has been widely quoted as stating that "stress will be the health epidemic of the twenty-first century."

It can be strange to see mind training—going nowhere, in effect—being brought to such forward-pushing worlds; the businesses that view retreats as the best way to advance may simply be deploying new and imaginative means to the same unelevated ends. To me, the point of sitting still is that it helps you see through the very idea of pushing forward; indeed, it strips you of yourself, as of a coat of armor, by leading you into a place where you're defined by something larger. If it does have benefits, they lie within some invisible account with a high interest rate but very long-term yields, to be drawn upon at that moment, surely inevitable, when a doctor walks into your room, shaking his head, or another car veers in front of yours, and all you have to draw upon is what you've collected in your deeper moments. But there's no questioning the need for clarity and focus, especially when the stakes are highest.

One spring morning, I heard a knock on my door in the monastery that had become my secret home—located only a couple of hours' drive from Silicon Valley—and opened it up to find two young friends I'd never met before but had come to know a little through correspondence. Emma was the associate director of a research center at Stanford, and her fiancé (now husband), Andrew, was a Marine. We walked down to a small bench overlooking the blue expanse of the Pacific—no islands in front of us, no oil rigs, no whales—and Emma explained how, as a postdoc in Wisconsin, she'd spent a year raising money to fund a study to see if military veterans facing the possibility of posttraumatic stress disorder could be helped by some training in stillness.

The guys who came into her lab, she said, were—as I would expect—hard-drinking, tattoo-covered, motorbike-riding Midwestern men who had no interest at all in what they called "hippie dipshit." As far as they were concerned, she was the one being tested, not they. But then she put ten of them through a weeklong yoga-based breathing program. And when they came out of the twenty-five-hour course in going nowhere, the veterans reported significant decreases in symptoms of stress, feelings of anxiety, and even respiration rate. The ten who didn't receive the training were unchanged.

As a professional scientist, she trusted only what could be empirically backed up, so she checked the veterans' startle reflex—unusually powerful, as a rule, in hypervigilant veterans and often the cause of sleeplessness and exaggerated fear responses—and discovered that the figures chimed exactly with the veterans' subjective accounts to her. More than one of them had taken her aback by saying she had literally brought him back from the dead. She tested her sample group a second time a week after the program—and then again a year later—and the improvements held up. Her paper describing the pilot study had been peer-reviewed and accepted by the *Journal of Traumatic Stress*.

Then Andrew spoke. He remained where he was, straight-backed and alert, standing beside the bench on which Emma and I were sitting, and began by confessing, with a polite smile, that meditation practice was never going to be an easy sell in the "alpha-male, hypermacho" world of the Marine Corps. In fact, when he'd embarked upon his own very strict forty-day program in sitting still, "I was more out to prove it wrong, or just to be my disciplined Marine self and see the mission through." But soon, to his surprise, he found his hours of concentrated attention were making him unusually happy, to the point where he began to worry he was losing his edge.

His adviser assured him that he was no less alert than before, just more selective about the "potential threats or targets to respond to. Which allowed me," Andrew went on, "to ignore many of the things I would normally pay attention to and to enjoy daily life more instead." He was amazed, as a hard-charging Marine Corps Scout Sniper, "that something this simple could be so powerful. And something so soft could also make me so much harder as a Marine."

Once, he said, a buddy of his had been the officer in charge in the last Humvee in a convoy in Afghanistan. The vehicle rolled over an explosive device, and the lower parts of both the man's legs had been instantly destroyed. But—thanks to his training in "tactical breathing"—the officer had found the presence of mind to check on the others around him, to ask his driver to signal for help, and, remarkably, to tourniquet what remained of his legs and keep them propped up until help could arrive. By altering his breathing and keeping still, according to a system he'd read about in a book for active service members, he'd saved his own life and those of many around him.

No one could say it was a panacea, and I have never been one for New Age ideas. It was the ideas of old age— or at least of those whose thoughts had stood the test of time for centuries, even millennia—that carried more authority for me. But twenty-two veterans are taking their own lives around us every day, and their average age is twenty-five. It doesn't seem crazy to think that training minds might help save lives at least as much as training bodies does.

5 A Secular Sabbath

The need for an empty space, a pause, is something we have all felt in our bones; it's the rest in a piece of music that gives it resonance and shape. That's the reason American football players prefer to go into a huddle rather than just race toward the line of scrimmage, the reason a certain kind of writer will include a lot of blank space on a page, so his sentences have room to breathe (and his readers, too). The one word for which the adjective "holy" is used in the Ten Commandments is Sabbath.

In the book of Numbers, God actually condemns to death a man found collecting wood on the Sabbath. The book on the Sabbath is the longest one in the Torah, as Judith Shulevitz explains in her fine work, *The Sabbath World*. Another part of the Torah, dealing with the Sabbath's boundaries, takes up 105 pages more.

Keeping the Sabbath—doing nothing for a while—is one of the hardest things in life for me; I'd much rather give up meat or wine or sex than the ability to check my e-mails or get on with my work when I want to. If I don't answer my messages today, I tell myself, there will only be more to answer tomorrow (though, in truth, refraining from sending messages will likely diminish the number I receive); if I take time off, I somehow believe, I'll be that much more hurried the rest of the time.

Whenever I finally force myself away from my desk for a day, of course, I find the opposite: the more time I spend away from my work, the better that work will be, most often.

One day Mahatma Gandhi was said to have woken up and told those around him, "This is going to be a very busy day. I won't be able to meditate for an hour." His friends were taken aback at this rare break from his discipline. "I'll have to meditate for two," he spelled out.

I mentioned this once on a radio program and a woman called in, understandably impatient. "It's all very well for a male travel writer in Santa Barbara to talk about taking time off," she said. "But what about me? I'm a mother trying to start a small business, and I don't have the luxury of meditating for two hours a day." Yet it's precisely those who are busiest, I wanted to tell her, who most need to give themselves a break. Stress is contagious, studies have found. If only the poor, overburdened mother could ask her husband—or her mother or a friend—to look after her kids for thirty minutes a day, I'm sure she'd have much more freshness and delight to share with her children when she came back, and with her business.

Some people, if they can afford it, try to acquire a place in the country or a second home; I've always thought it easier to make a second house in the week—especially if, like most of us, you lack the funds for expensive real estate. These days, in the age of movement and connection, space, as Marx had it in another context, has been annihilated by time; we feel as though we can make contact with almost anywhere at any moment. But as fast as geography is coming under our control, the clock is exerting more and more tyranny over us. And the more we can contact others, the more, it sometimes seems, we lose contact with ourselves. When I left New York City for the backstreets of Japan, I figured I'd be growing poorer in terms of money, amusements, social life, and obvious prospects, but I'd be richer in what I prize most: days and hours.

This is what the principle of the Sabbath enshrines. It is, as Abraham Joshua Heschel, the great Jewish theologian of the last century, had it, "a cathedral in time rather than in space"; the one day a week we take off becomes a vast empty space through which we can wander, without agenda, as through the light-filled passageways of Notre Dame. Of course, for a religious person, it's also very much about community and ritual and refreshing one's relationship with God and ages past. But even for the rest of us, it's like a retreat house that ensures we'll have something bright and purposeful to carry back into the other six days.

The Sabbath recalls to us that, in the end, all our journeys have to bring us home. And we do not have to travel far to get away from our less considered habits. The places that move us most deeply, as I found in the monastery, are often the ones we recognize like long-lost friends; we come to them with a piercing sense of familiarity, as if returning to some source we already know. "Some keep the Sabbath going to Church—" Emily Dickinson wrote. "I keep it, staying at Home."

●   ●   ●

One day, a year after meeting Matthieu Ricard and hearing how a transatlantic flight could be a "retreat in the sky," I found myself on such a flight, from Frankfurt to Los Angeles. The woman who came and sat next to me was young, very attractive and, as I would learn, from Germany. As she settled into her seat, she exchanged a few friendly words and then proceeded to sit in silence, doing nothing, for the next twelve hours.

I slept and paged through a novel, squeezed past her to go to the bathroom, and scrolled through options on the monitor before me, but she just sat there, never nodding off, yet apparently very much at peace. After we commenced our descent, I finally summoned the courage to ask her if she lived in LA.

No, she said, she was a social worker, and her job was exhausting. Now she was on her way to five weeks of vacation in Hawaii, the perfect antidote to her life in Berlin. But she liked to use the flight over to begin to get all the stress out of her system so that she could arrive on the islands in as clear a state as possible, ready to enjoy her days of rest.

I was humbled. So often I see vacations as just a way to direct my work habits and relentlessness toward mapping out schedules and organizing train tickets, less concerned with the quality of my time than the quantity. A flight for me had always been a chance to catch up on job-related reading, to see movies I'd never been tempted to see when they were playing at the Cineplex, to organize myself as fanatically as I do when at my desk. When Matthieu Ricard had given me his vision of taking a mini-Sabbath in the skies, I'd assumed that this was something available to a monk who'd meditated for three decades in the Himalayas, and not the rest of us.

But the next time I was flying home—from New York to California—I tried to take a page out of my former seatmate's near-empty book. I didn't turn on my monitor. I didn't race through a novel. I didn't even consciously try to do nothing: when an idea came to me or I recalled something I had to do back home, I pulled out a notebook and scribbled it down. The rest of the time, I just let my mind go foraging—or lie down—like a dog on a wide, empty beach.

It was three a.m. on the wristwatch I hadn't reset when I arrived home, but I felt as clear and refreshed as when, in the hour before sleeping, I choose not to scroll through YouTube or pick up a book but simply turn off all the lights and let some music wash over me. When I awoke the next morning, I felt as new as the world I looked out upon.

6 Coming Back Home

With every return to Nowhere, one can begin to discern its features, and with them its possibilities, a little more clearly. The place has moods and seasons as rich as the pulsing, red-dirt spaces of Australia's outback, as varied as the clouds you can see in a James Turrell Skyspace. Very often, I'll sit for weeks composing a work such as this one, making an outline, a linear A-B-C guide. The longer I sit still, however, the more those logical structures get turned inside out, till something beyond me is propelling me out of Nowhere down an entirely unexpected sequence of Q-C-A. I think of the time when I was on a boat in the Pacific and a biologist set up a device that allowed us to hear what was going on beneath us. Under the still blue waters, it turned out, was an uproar as scratchily cacophonous as Grand Central Station at rush hour. Stillness has nothing to do with settledness or stasis.

"One of the strange laws of the contemplative life," Thomas Merton, one of its sovereign explorers, pointed out, "is that in it you do not sit down and solve problems: you bear with them until they somehow solve themselves. Or until life solves them for you." Or, as Annie Dillard, who sat still for a long time at Tinker Creek—and in many other places—has it, "I do not so much write a book as sit up with it, as with a dying friend."

It's only by taking myself away from clutter and distraction that I can begin to hear something out of earshot and recall that listening is much more invigorating than giving voice to all the thoughts and prejudices that anyway keep me company twenty-four hours a day. And it's only by going nowhere—by sitting still or letting my mind relax—that I find that the thoughts that come to me unbidden are far fresher and more imaginative than the ones I consciously seek out. Setting an autoresponse on my e-mail, turning off the TV when I'm on the treadmill, trying to find a quiet place in the midst of a crowded day (or city)—all quickly open up an unsuspected space.

• • •

It takes courage, of course, to step out of the fray, as it takes courage to do anything that's necessary, whether tending to a loved one on her deathbed or turning away from that sugarcoated doughnut. And with billions of our global neighbors in crying need, with so much in every life that has to be done, it can sound selfish to take a break or go off to a quiet place. But as soon as you do sit still, you find that it actually brings you closer to others, in both understanding and sympathy. As the meditative video artist Bill Viola notes, it's the man who steps away from the world whose sleeve is wet with tears for it.

In any case, few of us have the chance to step out of

our daily lives often, or for very long; Nowhere has to become somewhere we visit in the corners of our lives by taking a daily run or going fishing or just sitting quietly for thirty minutes every morning (a mere 3 percent of our waking hours). The point of gathering stillness is not to enrich the sanctuary or mountaintop but to bring that calm into the motion, the commotion of the world.

Indeed, Nowhere can itself often become a routine, a treadmill, the opposite of something living, if you don't see it as a way station: sometimes during his days on Mount Baldy, Leonard Cohen would get into his car, drive down from the mountain, and stop off for a Filet-O-Fish at McDonald's. Then, suitably fortified, he'd go back to his house in one of the more forgotten parts of central Los Angeles and stretch out in front of *The Jerry Springer Show* on TV.

After a day or two, having gotten the restlessness out of his system—and recalling, perhaps, why he'd wanted to go up the mountain in the first place—he would drive back, but never with a view to staying there forever. Though always faithful to his friend Sasaki, who lived to 107, Cohen had begun traveling to Mumbai to hear a retired bank manager talk about the place behind our self-contradictory ideas where notions of "you" and "me" dissolve; he'd taken to writing about traffic jams and Babylon again, and, fleeing every pretense of unworldliness or sanctity, he'd gone back full-time into the modest home he shares with his daughter and taken on a beautiful young companion.

At the age of seventy-three, Cohen launched a global concert tour that continued for six years, taking him from Hanging Rock in Australia to Ljubljana, from Saskatoon to Istanbul. He gave more than three hundred concerts in all, nearly every one lasting more than three hours.

I went to see him onstage as the tour began and felt as if the whole spellbound crowd was witnessing something of the monastery, the art that stillness deepens. Much of the time the singer stood motionless near the back of the stage, hat doffed, almost invisible, as if back in the meditation hall. Other times he was all but down on his knees, squeezing every last drop out of each confession or prayer. It was a remarkable thing to see a man in his midseventies summon such stillness and furious energy, such collectedness and openness about his longings and his panic.

In 2012, something even stranger happened: a new record came out with the decidedly unsexy title of *Old Ideas*. Nearly all the songs on it were slow to the point of being stationary and dealt with darkness or suffering or the leaden heart of a man who's "got no taste for anything at all." As with most of the singer's recent albums, all the tunes were really about death, saying good-bye not just to a young woman but to everything he loved, not least life itself.

One day I woke up in a hotel in the LA Live entertainment zone, a glittery new complex of singles bars and megascreens, high-rising towers and a concert hall. I went downstairs to collect my morning Awake tea and heard, from the album being featured in the coffeehouse that week, a seventy-seven-year-old Zen monk croaking about "going home" to a place that sounded very much like death.

Old Ideas, rather astonishingly, had gone to the top of the charts already in seventeen countries and hit the Top Five in nine others. The singer's cold and broken "Hallelujah" had recently occupied the number one, number two, and number thirty-six spots in the British Top 40 simultaneously and become the fastest-selling download in European history. Long past what looked like retirement age, Leonard Cohen had suddenly become the latest thing, the prince of fashion, once again.

Why were people across the planet reaching out for such a funereal album with such an antitopical title? I wondered. Maybe they were finding a clarity and wisdom in the words of someone who'd gone nowhere, sitting still to look at the truth of the world and himself, that they didn't get from many other recording artists? Cohen seemed to be bringing us bulletins from somewhere more rooted than the CNN newsroom, and to be talking to us, as the best friends do, without varnish or evasion or design. And why were so many hastening to concerts delivered by a monk in his late seventies? Perhaps they longed to be taken back to a place of trust—which is what Nowhere is, at heart—where they could speak and listen with something deeper than their social selves and be returned to a penetrating intimacy.

In an age of speed, I began to think, nothing could be more invigorating than going slow.

In an age of distraction, nothing can feel more luxurious than paying attention.

And in an age of constant movement, nothing is more urgent than sitting still.

You can go on vacation to Paris or Hawaii or New Orleans three months from now, and you'll have a tremendous time, I'm sure. But if you want to come back feeling new—alive and full of fresh hope and in love with the world—I think the place to visit may be Nowhere.

ACKNOWLEDGMENTS

I'm deeply happy and honored to be involved in one of the first TED Originals; I fell into the TED orbit barely a year ago and instantly felt I was among bright, fun, and deeply committed kindred spirits who saw all kinds of fresh ways for bringing our world to new life. I owe heartfelt thanks to Chris Anderson and Bruno Giussani at TED for bringing me into the fold, and to all the others who have worked so hard to build a community, advance a vision, throw a terrific party, and share ideas we might not otherwise get to hear.

In the context of this book, I owe especial thanks to June Cohen, one of TED's longtime inspirations, and to my editor, Michelle Quint, for bringing such invigorating enthusiasm and such a beautifully clarifying and tenacious eye to my every comma. I would also like to thank Susan Lehman, who originally came up with the idea for this book (and who regularly seems to know what I should be writing about even when I do not), and Benjamin Holmes, for his meticulous and sympathetic copyedit. It was amazing to have Chip Kidd, a longtime colleague and friend from afar, bring his inimitable eye and vision to our cover, while Eydís Einarsdóttir's images from one of my favorite places on earth deepened and illuminated the atmosphere I was trying to catch in my text.

I always owe huge thanks to my steadfast, brilliant friend and agent, Lynn Nesbit, and to Michael Steger at Janklow & Nesbit, for looking out for me—for all of us—in ways so human, so discerning, and so kind. And it must be clear how much I owe various friends and inspirations, some of them (Proust and Thoreau, Thomas Merton and Emily Dickinson) never quite met in the flesh, some of them (Leonard Cohen and Annie Dillard, Matthieu Ricard and the Fourteenth Dalai Lama) glimpsed here and there.

Thank you, finally, to the monks and oblates and fellow wanderers who pass through the New Camaldoli Hermitage, so open and forbearing even though I regularly do so little justice to their lives.

The images in this book were all taken by Icelandic/Canadian photographer Eydís S. Luna Einarsdóttir. They have not been digitally altered, beyond standard color correction.

Einarsdóttir began her visual journey at a young age, influenced by her father—an avid photographer—her artist mother, and the Icelandic light and landscape. Detail, contrast, and simplicity best describe her photography. Her subtle grasp of color and talent for lighting create an alluring and visually distinctive edge.

ARTIST'S STATEMENT

Stillness, or, in Icelandic, *kyrrð*—the word itself brings me right back to one of the few places I have ever found perfect stillness in mind and body: Iceland.

Every year I travel from my home in Vancouver, Canada, to Iceland, the place of my birth. I don't stay in the city much; instead, I head out to my parents' quiet lakeside cabin to take a rest from the self-imposed stress of my life and to experience *kyrrð og ró* (peace and quiet).

After a couple of days of recuperation, my parents and I head out on excursions around the island. To me these travels are not so much a photographic exploration as a time to visit with my parents and my "old" country; the camera simply comes along. However, with the breathtaking views and beautiful light Iceland offers, a stop here and there is inevitable.

As soon as I take out my camera I find that stillness within, that deep sense of peace that I crave every day. I get lost in such a beautiful way that it's hard to describe; it's as though I find a piece of me that I had lost without really knowing that I lost it. As I sit quietly looking through the viewfinder, my senses become heightened. The smell of the earth makes me feel grounded; the sound of waves crashing or grass rustling in the wind or the bleating of a lone sheep in the distance makes me feel so alive; and the vastness of what I see makes me feel expansive. This is what it is like to be in the Now, which is really just to be still in mind and body. My photographs come from a place of emotion. They are not an attempt to capture the perfect image, but to capture the feeling I experience as I witness the things in front of me.

ABOUT THE AUTHOR

PICO IYER has been traveling the world for more than forty years now, from Easter Island to Bhutan and Ethiopia to Los Angeles Airport. His descriptions of those journeys have appeared in such books as *Video Night in Kathmandu*, *The Lady and the Monk*, *The Global Soul*, and *The Open Road*, and he's written novels about Revolutionary Cuba and Islam. For twenty years he's been a constant contributor to *The New York Times*, *The New York Review of Books*, *Harper's*, *Time*, and scores of other magazines and newspapers across the globe. He currently serves as a Distinguished Presidential Fellow at Chapman University.

Pico Iyer's 14-minute talk, available for free at TED.com, is the companion to *The Art of Stillness*.

TED.com/stillness

PHOTO: JAMES DUNCAN DAVIDSON

RELATED TALKS ON TED.COM

Pico Iyer: *Where is home?*
go.ted.com/Iyer

More and more people worldwide are living in countries not considered their own. Pico Iyer—who himself has three or four "origins"—meditates on the joy of traveling and the meaning of home.

Carl Honore: *In praise of slowness*
go.ted.com/Honore

Journalist Carl Honore believes the Western world's emphasis on speed erodes health, productivity and quality of life. But there's a backlash brewing, as everyday people start putting the brakes on their all-too-modern lives.

Matthieu Ricard: *The habits of happiness*
go.ted.com/Ricard

What is happiness, and how can we all get some? Biochemist turned Buddhist monk Matthieu Ricard says we can train our minds in habits of well-being, to generate a true sense of serenity and fulfillment.

Louie Schwartzberg: *Nature. Beauty. Gratitude.*
go.ted.com/Schwartzberg

Louie Schwartzberg's stunning time-lapse photography—accompanied by powerful words from Benedictine monk Brother David Steindl-Rast—serves as a meditation on being grateful for every day.

TED is a nonprofit devoted to spreading ideas, usually in the form of short, powerful talks (18 minutes or less) but also through books, animation, radio programs, and events. TED began in 1984 as a conference where Technology, Entertainment and Design converged, and today covers almost every topic—from science to business to global issues—in more than 100 languages.

TED is a global community, welcoming people from every discipline and culture who seek a deeper understanding of the world. We believe passionately in the power of ideas to change attitudes, lives and, ultimately, our future. On TED.com, we're building a clearinghouse of free knowledge from the world's most inspired thinkers—and a community of curious souls to engage with ideas and each other. Our annual flagship conference convenes thought leaders from all fields to exchange ideas. Our TEDx program allows communities worldwide to host their own independent, local events, all year long. And our Open Translation Project ensures these ideas can move across borders.

In fact, everything we do—from the TED Radio Hour to the projects sparked by the TED Prize, from TEDx events to the TED-Ed lesson series—is driven by this goal: How can we best spread great ideas?

TED is owned by a nonprofit, nonpartisan foundation.